50 Shared texts

Photocopiable texts for shared reading

- Fiction, non-fiction and poetry
- Annotated versions
- Discussion prompts

Sue Taylor

Credits

Author
Sue Taylor

Illustrations
David Ashby

Series Consultants
Fiona Collins and
Alison Kelly

Series Designer
Anna Oliwa

Editor
Dulcie Booth

Designer
Anna Oliwa

Assistant Editor
Roanne Charles

Text © 2004 Sue Taylor
© 2004 Scholastic Ltd

Designed using Adobe InDesign

Published by Scholastic Ltd
Villiers House
Clarendon Avenue
Leamington Spa
Warwickshire CV32 5PR

www.scholastic.co.uk

Printed by Bell & Bain Ltd, Glasgow

1 2 3 4 5 6 7 8 9   4 5 6 7 8 9 0 1 2 3

British Library Cataloguing-in-Publication Data
A catalogue record for this book is available from the British Library.

ISBN 0-439-98480-7

The right of Sue Taylor to be identified as the author of this work has been asserted by her in accordance with the Copyright, Designs and Patents Act 1988.

Contents

Introduction 5

Range and objectives 7

Term 1

	N	**P**
But you promised!	**10**	**110**
A List	**12**	**111**
The Rare Spotted Birthday Party	**14**	**112**
The Magic Finger	**16**	**113**
The Werepuppy	**18**	**114**
I'm not scared of the monster ..	**20**	**115**
Don't	**22**	**116**
Dinner-time Rhyme	**24**	**117**
Best Friends	**26**	**118**
What is the sun?	**28**	**119**
Dad	**30**	**120**
Chewy Chocolate Crunch Cakes	**32**	**121**

	N	**P**
The concertina book	**34**	**122**
Following directions	**36**	**123**
Felt finger puppets	**38**	**124**
How to play Boxes	**40**	**125**

Term 2

	N	**P**
Little Red Riding Hood (extract 1)	**42**	**126**
Little Red Riding Hood (extract 2)	**44**	**127**
Brer Rabbit and the Tar Baby (extract 1)	**46**	**128**
Brer Rabbit and the Tar Baby (extract 2)	**48**	**129**
Rabbit and Tiger	**50**	**130**
The Little Red Hen and the Grain of Wheat	**52**	**131**
Come-day Go-day	**54**	**132**

N *Teacher's notes*   **P** *Photocopiable*

Term 2 *continued*   N   P

The End and Happiness
(poems 1 & 2) 56   133

Morning 58   134

Caribbean Counting Rhyme 60   135

Word of a Lie 62   136

Conversation 64   137

Dictionary entries 66   138

Synonyms 68   139

Glossary and Index
(extracts 1 & 2) 70   140

Butterflies and Moths 72   141

How flowers grow 74   142

Term 3

Book blurbs (extracts 1 & 2) ..... N   P

Story openings
(extracts 1 & 2) 78   144

Scene setting
(extracts 1 & 2) 80   145

     N   P

Characterisation
(extracts 1 & 2) 82   146

Little Red Riding Pig 84   147

The Really Ugly Duckling 86   148

A Big Bare Bear 88   149

On the Ning Nang Nong 90   150

Sneezles 92   151

Busy Day 94   152

Limericks 96   153

Teaser 98   154

Barry and Beryl the Bubble
Gum Blowers 100 155

Fact or fiction? 102 156

Dolphins and Porpoises 104 157

Our Solar System 106 158

Pushing and pulling 108 159

Acknowledgements 160

N *Teacher's notes*   P *Photocopiable*

Introduction

In *50 Shared texts* you will find a range of texts for use in shared reading. In recent years shared text work has become the focal point of daily literacy work, and the success of such shared work is clearly linked to the quality and choice of text. Better understanding of children's reading and writing development has led to the realisation that a greater range of text types, or genres, is needed to enrich children's literacy development. For the busy classroom teacher, seeking out such a range of quality texts can be too time-consuming, which is why appropriate texts have been provided in this book.

Shared reading

Shared reading is at the heart of the activities in this book and is a cornerstone of the National Literacy Strategy, which states that through shared reading children *begin to recognise important characteristics of a variety of written texts, often linked to style and voice.*

First developed in New Zealand by Don Holdaway, shared reading has been a significant literacy routine for children since the 1980s. Holdaway's research and pioneering work in schools brought the benefits of sharing enlarged texts or Big Books to teachers' attention. From his observations of very young children attending to bedtime stories on a one-to-one basis he realised that a similar intimacy with print could be offered through sharing an enlarged text with a group or class of children. He showed how engagement with Big Books can teach children about the characteristics of different text types, their organisation and distinguishing features, as well as the finer details of print. For example, depending on the teacher's focus, an enlarged recipe could be used at text level to model the way a piece of instructional writing is structured, at sentence level to look at the use of imperative verbs or at word level to focus on a particular phoneme. In relation to literature, the meaning of a poem can be explored at text level, the poet's choice of verbs at sentence level and the rhyming pattern at word level. So, shared reading not only encourages the class to share the actual reading aloud of a text but also enables the teacher to discuss certain language features and support the children in both comprehending and responding to the text.

With younger children, shared reading involves following the text with a pointer to highlight key early concepts of print such as directionality and one-to-one correspondence. With such concepts securely in place, a rather different technique is needed for older children where the focus shifts more to understanding and responding to the text as well as discussing vocabulary and linguistic features. For all children, often the talk surrounding the reading is as important as the reading itself.

Finding the right quality texts for shared reading that will engage and interest the children, as well as meeting the many NLS objectives, can be a difficult task. Once a text is found, you need to identify salient features at word, sentence and text level.

Shared reading is also the springboard for shared writing, guided reading/writing and independent work. Both guided reading and writing provide opportunities for you to guide, support, model and comment on children's response to a text. Activities may involve reading aloud, role-play, performance or writing for a particular purpose. Independent activities may mirror these but need to be clearly structured to enable the children to work independently.

About this book

The texts in this book are organised term by term, following the NLS framework, so there are examples of fiction, poetry, plays and non-fiction.

For each text, both a blank and annotated version are provided. The former is for use with children and can either be enlarged or projected on an overhead projector; the latter is for teacher information and identifies the features of the text and links with NLS objectives.

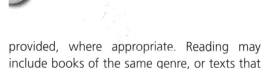

Background

Background information is provided for each text. This will contextualise the extract, fill in any necessary details and give facts about its author as relevant. Information on themes, technical features or other related texts might also feature here.

Shared reading and discussing the text

This section offers guidance on ways of managing discussion around the text, as well as ways of organising the shared reading. Depending on the age of the children, and demands of the text, different strategies for working with the whole class on the text are given, as well as ways of triggering the children's responses. These include structured discussion suggestions, ideas for role-play, and performance techniques.

Activities

Building on the reading and discussion, this section suggests activities for both whole-class work and guided or independent group work. There are ideas for further textual analysis, sometimes involving shared writing. As in the previous section, talk is pivotal in developing the children's understanding.

Extension/further reading

Suggestions for taking activities into a broader context and ideas for linked reading are also provided, where appropriate. Reading may include books of the same genre, or texts that share the theme or the same author.

The texts

The choice of texts has been driven by the need to ensure that these are quality texts both in content and language. It is hoped that among the selection you will find a mixture of authors and texts, both familiar and new. Whole texts have been provided as far as possible so that children have the satisfaction of reading and appreciating a coherent and complete piece of writing.

Longer texts, such as novels, also need to feature in older children's reading, and sometimes more than one extract from the same carefully chosen novel has been included. Bearing in mind that children should experience as much of the novel as they can, it is recommended that you use the background notes to fill the children in on plot detail, and that you read the story to them or have copies, including a taped version, available for their own reading or listening. Other slots in the curriculum can be used for such reading: private reading, homework, independent group work or story time.

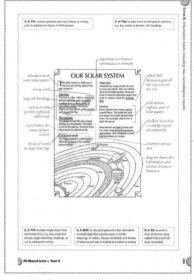

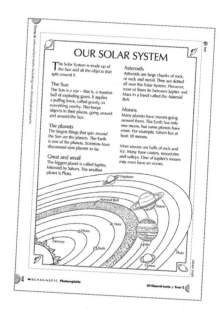

Range and objectives

Year 2 Term 1

Range	Text	NLS references
Stories with familiar settings	**'But you promised!'** from *But you promised!* by Bel Mooney (Egmont)	S3, S5, T5, T6, T10
	'A List' from *Frog and Toad Together* by Arnold Lobel (Egmont)	W1, W3, W4, W5, T1, T4, T11
	'The Rare Spotted Birthday Party' by Margaret Mahy from *A Treasury of Stories for Five Year Olds* chosen by Edward and Nancy Blishen (Kingfisher)	W3, S4, T5, T6, T10
	'The Magic Finger' from *The Magic Finger* by Roald Dahl (Puffin Books)	S2, S5, T3, T4, T10
	'The Werepuppy' from *The Werepuppy on Holiday* by Jacqueline Wilson (Puffin Books)	S3, S6, T3, T5
Poems with familiar settings	**'I'm not scared of the monster'** from *Bare Bear and other rhymes* by John Foster (Oxford University Press)	W4, S5, T7, T8
	'Don't' by John Kitching from *Twinkle Twinkle Chocolate Bar* compiled by John Foster (Oxford University Press)	W4, T7, T8, T12
	'Dinner-time Rhyme' from *Jungle Sale* by June Crebbin (Viking)	W3, T7, T8, T12
	'Best Friends' by Bernard Young from *Poems About You and Me* compiled by Brian Moses (Hodder Wayland)	S6, T6, T7, T12
	'What is the sun?' from *Read a Poem, Write a Poem* by Wes Magee (Basil Blackwell)	W7, W9, T7, T8, T12
	'Dad' from *Walking on Air* by Berlie Doherty (HarperCollins)	S3, S4, S6, T7, T12
Instructions	**'Chewy Chocolate Crunch Cakes'** by Sue Taylor	S5, T13, T14
	'The concertina book' from *Children Making Books* by Paul Johnson (Reading and Language Information Centre)	S2, T11, T15, T16, T17
	'Following directions' by Sue Taylor	S2, S6, T13, T14, T15, T16
	'Felt finger puppets' from *Making Puppets* by Josie McKinnon (Rigby Educational)	T13, T14, T16, T17
	'How to play Boxes' by Sue Taylor	S4, T13, T14, T15, T17

Year 2 Term 2

Range	Text	NLS references
Traditional stories	**'Little Red Riding Hood'** (extract 1) from *The Helen Oxenbury Nursery Story Book* by Helen Oxenbury (Egmont)	W4, S3, T2, T4, T5, T13
	'Little Red Riding Hood' (extract 2) from *The Helen Oxenbury Nursery Story Book* by Helen Oxenbury (Egmont)	W2, T3, T6, T14
Traditional stories from other cultures	**'Brer Rabbit and the Tar Baby'** (extract 1) from *The Tales of Uncle Remus* retold by Julius Lester (Puffin Books)	W5, S2, S4, T3, T4, T6, T14
	'Brer Rabbit and the Tar Baby' (extract 2) from *The Tales of Uncle Remus* retold by Julius Lester (Puffin Books)	S5, T4, T7, T14
	'Rabbit and Tiger' from *Cric Crac* by Grace Hallworth (Mammoth)	S3, S9, T5, T7, T13
Traditional stories with predictable and patterned language	**'The Little Red Hen and the Grain of Wheat'** retold by Sara Cone Bryant from *The Fairy Tale Treasury* selected by Virgina Haviland (Random House)	S2, S6, S7, T7
Poems with predictable and patterned language	**'Come-day Go-day'** by Barrie Wade from *Twinkle Twinkle Chocolate Bar* compiled by John Foster (Oxford University Press)	W1, W2, W9, T8, T9, T15
	'The End' from *Now We Are Six* by AA Milne and **'Happiness'** from *When We Were Very Young* by AA Milne (both Methuen)	W6, S5, T9, T11, T15
Poems from other cultures; poems with predictable and patterned language	**'Morning'** from *Give Yourself a Hug* by Grace Nichols (Puffin Books)	W4, W5, T8, T9, T10, T15
	'Caribbean Counting Rhyme' by Pamela Mordecai from *Twinkle Twinkle Chocolate Bar* compiled by John Foster (Oxford University Press)	W5, W6, T5, T9, T10, T15
Poems with predictable and patterned language; poems by significant children's poets	**'Word of a Lie'** from *The Frog Who Dreamed She Was an Opera Singer* by Jackie Kay (Bloomsbury)	S8, T8, T10, T11, T15
	'Conversation' from *Wouldn't You Like to Know* by Michael Rosen (Scholastic)	W3, S6, T8, T11, T15
Dictionaries	**'Dictionary entries'** from *Collins Junior Dictionary* (HarperCollins)	W8, W11, S7, T16, T17
Alphabetically ordered texts	**'Synonyms'** from *Collins Junior Dictionary* (HarperCollins)	W8, W11, T18
Glossaries and indexes	**'Glossary'** and **'Index'** from *Butterflies and Moths* by Sally Morgan (Chrysalis Children's Books)	W10, T16, T17, T18, T20
Explanations	**'Butterflies and Moths'** from *Butterflies and Moths* by Sally Morgan (Chrysalis Children's Books)	W10, S7, T19, T20, T21
	'How flowers grow' from *Finding Out About Everyday Things* by Eliot Humberstone (Usborne)	W10, S7, T19, T20, T21

Year 2 Term 3

Range	Text	NLS references
Extended stories by significant children's authors	**'Book blurbs'** from *The Hodgeheg* by Dick King-Smith (Puffin Books) and *The Otter Who Wanted to Know* by Jill Tomlinson (Egmont Books)	S2, T5, T7
	'Story openings' from *The Hodgeheg* by Dick King-Smith (Puffin Books) and *The Otter Who Wanted to Know* by Jill Tomlinson (Egmont Books)	W1, W2, W8, S1, S3, T1, T7, T9
	'Scene setting' from *The Hodgeheg* by Dick King-Smith (Puffin Books) and *The Otter Who Wanted to Know* by Jill Tomlinson (Egmont Books)	W10, T3, T7
	'Characterisation' from *The Hodgeheg* by Dick King-Smith (Puffin Books) and *The Otter Who Wanted to Know* by Jill Tomlinson (Egmont Books)	W7, T10, T12
Different stories by the same author; humorous stories	**'Little Red Riding Pig'** from *Dick King-Smith's Triffic Pig Book* by Dick King-Smith (Orion)	W10, T3, T4, T6
Humorous stories	**'The Really Ugly Duckling'** from *The Stinky Cheese Man and Other Fairly Stupid Tales* by Jon Scieszka (Puffin Books)	W7, S1, T6, T11
Texts with language play: humorous verse	**'A Big Bare Bear'** by Robert Heidbreder from *Twinkle Twinkle Chocolate Bar* compiled by John Foster (Oxford University Press)	W1, W3, W6, T6, T8
	'On the Ning Nang Nong' from *Silly Verse for Kids* by Spike Milligan (Puffin Books)	W2, T1, T6, T8, T11
	'Sneezles' from *Now We Are Six* by AA Milne (Methuen)	W1, W3, S1, T1, T6, T8
	'Busy Day' by Michael Rosen from *You Tell Me* by Roger McGough and Michael Rosen (Puffin Books)	S1, T6, T8, T11
	'Limericks' 1. by Edward Lear, 2. by John Kitching and 3. by Jack Ousbey from *The Works* chosen by Paul Cookson (Macmillan), 4. from *Read Me A Poem A Day For The National Year of Reading* edited by Gaby Morgan (Macmillan), 5. from *The Puffin Book of Fantastic First Poems* edited by June Crebbin	W2, S1, T6, T8, T11
Texts with language play: riddles, humorous verse	**'Teaser'** by Tony Mitton from *The Works* chosen by Paul Cookson (Macmillan)	S6, T6, T8, T11
Texts with language play: tongue-twisers	**'Barry and Beryl the Bubble Gum Blowers'** by Paul Cookson from *Tongue Twisters and Tonsil Twizzlers* chosen by Paul Cookson (Macmillan)	S1, T6, T8, T11
Information books	**'Fact or fiction?'**: extract 1 from *The Otter Who Wanted to Know* by Jill Tomlinson (Egmont Books); extracts 2 and 3 from *The Book of Whales, Dolphins and Porpoises* by Lionel Bender (Scholastic)	T13, T14, T15
Information books including non-chronological reports	**'Dolphins and Porpoises'** from *The Book of Whales, Dolphins and Porpoises* by Lionel Bender (Scholastic)	T13, T14, T16, T17, T18
	'Our Solar System' from *Our Solar System* by Alistair Smith (Usborne)	W10, S5, T14, T16, T19
	'Pushing and pulling' from *Forces and Movement* by Peter D Riley (Franklin Watts)	W9, T16, T19, T21

But you promised! by Bel Mooney

Background

This extract is taken from the fourth book in Bel Mooney's series which explores common childhood experiences, fears and complaints through a very believable heroine. *But you promised!* contains eight short stories on the theme of broken (and kept) promises, and is an accessible chapter book. The first chapter, of which this is an extract, describes the conflict between Kitty's desire for a pet and her mum's reservations, encouraging children to consider different points of view. The story allows children to make links to their own experiences – both of wanting something they cannot have and of broken promises. The author indicates characters' feelings in this extract in a variety of ways, giving the opportunity for close exploration of the vocabulary. The language is simple and direct, and the dialogue is natural, developing expressive reading aloud.

Shared reading and discussing the text

● Initially reveal only the title *But you promised!* Ask the children who might say this. Discuss the meaning and significance of promises. Is this about a promise that has been kept or one that has been broken? (Draw attention to *But*.)
● Now reveal the rest of the title … *I could have a pet.* Who do the children think wants a pet and who might have broken a promise?
● Now read the extract. Track the arguments running through the text – Kitty, Daniel, Mum, Dad – noting the reasons put forward by each character. Consider whether Mum's reasons are justifiable. Relate this to the children's own experiences and consider the responsibilities of adults. Consider Dad's difficult position and his point of view. Notice how Kitty manages to draw Dad onto her side! Have the children ever tried this with grown-ups – playing one against the other? *'Well…'* might suggest that Dad feels caught between Mum's position and the children's.
● Consider how each character feels, drawing attention to significant words and phrases (*cross, disappointed, guilty, 'Oh dear'*).

● Ask the children to predict what might happen next. Think about clues in the text – Mum's 'guilt', possibilities for compromise.
● Re-read the first four lines of the extract. Note devices that indicate how dialogue should be read – italic, capitalisation, exclamation marks and vocabulary (*wailed, firmly*). Explore other examples then re-read the extract, with groups or individuals taking character parts. Emphasise reading aloud with appropriate expression.

Activities

● Ask the children in pairs to think of another situation where a grown-up might break a promise to a child. Model the planning of one story (*But you promised… I could go to the park*). Why might a grown-up not keep his or her promise? (Fears about safety, for example.) What is the resolution? Remind the children of the possibilities for compromise (*We'll go together at the weekend*). In small groups, children can role-play a similar situation.
● Children could draw pictures for a storyboard on the situation they role-played above and use speech bubbles for dialogue.
● Rewrite the speech bubbles from the storyboard into dialogue, adding indications of how the dialogue should be read – using similar devices to the extract. Act as scribe for less confident children. More able writers can use speech marks to indicate dialogue.
● Children could write their own *But you promised…* stories, from different points of view and leading to different resolutions.

Extension/further reading

If the complete text is available, compare predictions made earlier with the actual story. Discuss the outcome. Do the children think everybody was happy? Was this a fair compromise? Look at other books in Bel Mooney's *Kitty* series as well as books which explore childhood experiences, for example Jill Tomlinson's *The Owl Who Was Afraid of the Dark* and *The Otter Who Wanted to Know.*

2: 1: T5: to identify and discuss reasons for events in stories, linked to plot

2: 1: T6: to discuss familiar story themes and link to own experiences, e.g. illness, getting lost, going away

2: 1: T10: to use story structure to write about own experience in same/ similar form

suggests that the promise has not been kept

indicate how characters speak

Kitty's feelings

Dad hesitant, caught in the middle

indication of Mum's own needs – another point of view

indication of Kitty's feelings – accepting defeat, suggesting alternative

mixed feelings

Dad again caught in the middle

emphasis

capitals for emphasis and volume

exclamation mark to indicate how to read

italics for emphasis

direct appeal to Dad to get him 'on side'

common argument made by children

in reality, although Kitty and Daniel may intend to take responsibility, it will fall to Mum

a soft toy, probably used by Kitty as her confidante in troubled times

shows how to read Kitty's speech aloud

But you promised!
…I could have a pet

"But you *promised* I could have a pet," wailed Kitty.

"No I didn't," said Mum firmly. "Not a proper promise. I just said…"

"You said I could have a dog for Christmas – you DID!"

Kitty was cross and disappointed. Mum and Dad had said she could have a pet for Christmas, and she and Daniel had decided a dog would be most fun. But now Mum had a job, and so she said it would be too much trouble. "I'll have so much to do, Kitty," she sighed. "You must understand."

But Kitty only understood one thing. "You *said* we'd get a dog, and Dad said he'd like one too, didn't you Dad?"

"Well, yes, I did," said Dad.

"I want us to have a pet. All the boys in school have animals. And I'd help Kitty look after it," said Daniel.

"But puppies need training, and dogs have to be taken for walks, and dog food has to be bought – and who'd do all that?" asked Mum. "I wanted this job so much, and it means I'll have less time to do all the things I have to do."

"What about a little kitten?" asked Kitty, in a small voice.

"I don't want extra chores," said Mum firmly. "I'm sorry." She sounded cross, but a bit guilty too.

Kitty looked furious.

Dan looked disappointed.

"Oh dear," said Dad.

Kitty turned and ran from the room, not minding that she made all the decorations on the tree shiver as she passed. Up in her room she picked up Mr Tubs and hugged him. "Grown-ups never keep their promises," she whispered. "So it looks as if we won't get our puppy, Mr T."

consider what might happen next, looking at clues – Mum feeling guilty, possibilities for compromise

2: 1: S3: to recognise and take account of commas and exclamation marks in reading aloud with appropriate expression

2: 1: S5: to revise knowledge about other uses of capitalisation, e.g. for names, headings, titles, emphasis, and begin to use in own writing

A List

by Arnold Lobel

Background

This extract comes from *Frog and Toad Together,* one of several books about the two friends and their everyday adventures, with which children can identify. Here, Toad makes a list to ensure that he remembers everything he has to do on a busy day, but the list blows away before he has done everything on it. The story offers a simple and explicit structure to develop children's concepts of time sequences in stories. The text includes many of the high-frequency words for Key Stage 1, and words containing a range of long-vowel phonemes.

Shared reading and discussing the text

● Begin by discussing the title and sharing experiences of lists and their purposes.

● Read the extract with the children. Discuss the purpose of Toad's list. Consider Toad's notion of *many things to do.* Would lists usually be made for those events that happen every day as a matter of course?

● Track the items on Toad's list against the events of the story. Note the chronological order. Discuss whether the list could be written or followed in any other order. Use the language of time to identify the sequence – what did Toad do *first*?

● Consider the question posed by Toad at the end. Predict what will happen. In shared writing, compose an ending to the story.

● Before re-reading the extract, cover some of the words with Post-it Notes – for example *remember, piece, paper, cupboard, opened, front, blew.* Model the use of a range of strategies to work out what the missing words are, such as re-reading the sentence, and ask children to explain how they know what the word is – developing use of context and grammar (*I know that clothes are kept in a cupboard* or *The missing word must describe Frog's door*).

● Highlight *Toad, wrote* and *blowing* in the text and draw attention to the common sound but different spellings. Brainstorm other words with the same phoneme and categorise spellings.

Repeat as necessary for the vowel phonemes *ee, ai, oo, ie* (compare *right* and *write*) from Year 1, and *ow* and short *oo* from Year 2.

Activities

● Give the children the list of events cut up and mixed up, to sequence and use to retell the story They can then go on to rewrite the story. Give less able children picture prompts with the list to assist sequencing, and let them retell orally rather than in writing. More able children can experiment with the time sequence, and consider how the story changes if events happen in a different order. You may wish to give this activity an ICT focus by cutting up text on screen for children to move and put in sequence.

● Children can make their own lists of 'things to do tomorrow', followed by writing a recount of their day, using the language of time. Less able writers can recount their day onto tape, or use a writing frame with time connectives, drawing a sequence of events first.

● Encourage pairs of children to develop reading and spelling of high-frequency words for Key Stage 1 (there are about 25 in this extract), using strategies such as matching cards or Look–Say–Cover–Write–Check.

● Ask the children to collect and categorise words containing long-vowel phonemes from their own reading.

Extension/further reading

Make links to instruction writing, looking at imperative verbs in the list. If the whole story is available, read the second part and compare the actual ending with the children's predictions. Other books in the same series will develop children's independent reading and encourage the use of the full range of strategies. Other stories with a clear and explicit time sequence include *Peace at Last* by Jill Murphy (Macmillan) and *Mr Gumpy's Motor Car* by John Burningham (Red Fox). *Mr Wolf's Pancakes* by Jan Fearnley (Picture Mammoth) also incorporates the theme of lists.

2: 1: T1: to reinforce and apply their word-level skills through shared and guided reading

2: 1: T4: to understand time and sequential relationships in stories, i.e. what happened when

2: 1: T11: to use language of time (see sentence level work) to structure a sequence of events, e.g. *'when I had finished...'*, *'suddenly...'*, *'after that...'*

2: 1: W1: to secure identification, spelling and reading of long-vowel digraphs in simple words from Y1 term 3 (the common spelling patterns for each long-vowel phoneme) – Appendix List 3

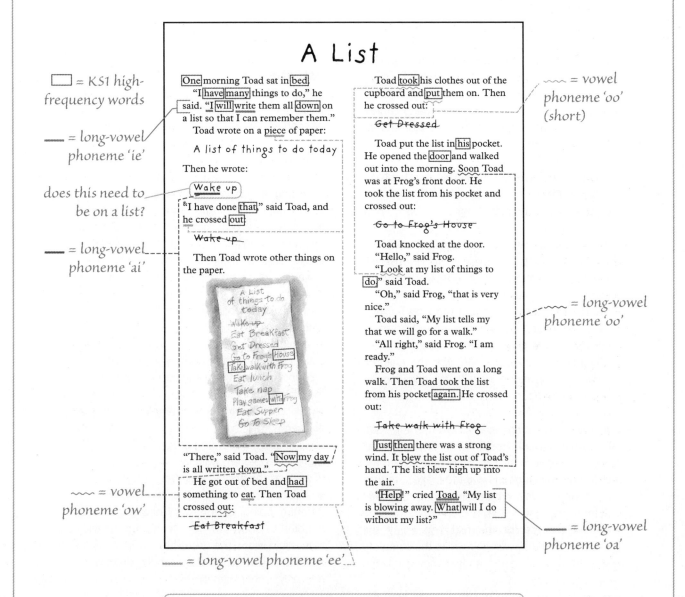

☐ = KS1 high-frequency words

―― = long-vowel phoneme 'ie'

does this need to be on a list?

―― = long-vowel phoneme 'ai'

〰 = vowel phoneme 'ow'

〰 = vowel phoneme 'oo' (short)

〰 = long-vowel phoneme 'oo'

―― = long-vowel phoneme 'oa'

―― = long-vowel phoneme 'ee'

A List

One morning Toad sat in bed.
"I have many things to do," he said. "I will write them all down on a list so that I can remember them."
Toad wrote on a piece of paper:

A list of things to do today

Then he wrote:

Wake up

"I have done that," said Toad, and he crossed out:

Wake up

Then Toad wrote other things on the paper.

A List of things to do today
Wake up
Eat Breakfast
Get Dressed
Go to Frog's House
Take walk with Frog
Eat lunch
Take nap
Play games with Frog
Eat Supper
Go To Sleep

"There," said Toad. "Now my day is all written down."
He got out of bed and had something to eat. Then Toad crossed out:

Eat Breakfast

Toad took his clothes out of the cupboard and put them on. Then he crossed out:

Get Dressed

Toad put the list in his pocket. He opened the door and walked out into the morning. Soon Toad was at Frog's front door. He took the list from his pocket and crossed out:

Go to Frog's House

Toad knocked at the door.
"Hello," said Frog.
"Look at my list of things to do," said Toad.
"Oh," said Frog, "that is very nice."
Toad said, "My list tells my that we will go for a walk."
"All right," said Frog. "I am ready."
Frog and Toad went on a long walk. Then Toad took the list from his pocket again. He crossed out:

Take walk with Frog

Just then there was a strong wind. It blew the list out of Toad's hand. The list blew high up into the air.
"Help!" cried Toad, "My list is blowing away. What will I do without my list?"

2: 1: W2: to revise and extend the reading and spelling of words containing different spellings of the long-vowel phonemes from Year 1

2: 1: W3: the common spelling patterns for the vowel phonemes: *'oo'* (short as in *good*), *'ar'*, *'oy'* *'ow'* (Appendix List 3):
● to identify the phonemes in speech and writing
● to blend the phonemes for reading
● to segment the words into phonemes for spelling

2: 1: W4: to investigate and classify words with the same sounds but different spellings

2: 1: W5: to read on sight and spell approximately 30 more words from Appendix List 1

The Rare Spotted Birthday Party

by Margaret Mahy

Background

Margaret Mahy describes hers as 'an ordinary life'. This may be why many of her stories for younger children are about everyday situations in familiar settings. In this story, Mark's birthday is two days away, but he has caught the measles and his planned birthday party cannot go ahead. The story encourages exploration of feelings through a familiar context.

Shared reading and discussing the text

● Cover the text and read the title. Ask the children what the story might be about. Why might a birthday party be *spotted*? (Bring out the connection with the rare spotted owl.)

● Read the first few lines, up to *He just felt spotty*. Consider again a possible storyline. Share experiences of being ill, particularly 'spotty' illnesses. How might Mark be feeling? Does this change? Encourage the children to refer directly to clues in the text.

● Read up to *special at all*. Ask the children how Mark is feeling now. Is he enjoying his birthday? Why not? What makes birthdays special?

● Now read to *measles from getting out*. Discuss why Mark's mother is brushing him all over for a drive in the car. Share times when the children's own mothers want to make sure they are clean and tidy. Where might they be going? Refer to the story's title.

● Read the rest of the text and enjoy the surprise! You may wish to re-read the complete text to give a better understanding of the whole extract.

● Ask the children to discuss in pairs how the surprise happened. Who do they think planned it? Refer to the clues in the text and identify and discuss reasons for the different events in the story. For example, Mark can't have a party because he is *infectious* (discuss this vocabulary); he wonders why his mum is tidying him up (she knows what's happening, but Mark doesn't and nor does the reader).

● Highlight *party*, *Mark* and *car*. Ask the children to focus on the phoneme common to the three words and identify the letters that represent it (*ar*). Brainstorm other words with the same phoneme and investigate spellings.

Activities

● Ask pairs of children to share times when they have felt disappointed (or frightened, worried and so on) about something which has subsequently turned out well. Share some experiences with the rest of the class. In shared writing, plan a recount of an experience, using a writing frame to outline the problem, the resolution, and feelings before and afterwards.

● Children can plan and then write their own recounts, using the frame from shared writing above. Less able children may need sentence starters, drawn from their plans – *It was my birthday and I felt miserable because…*

● In guided group work, ask the children to re-read their writing for sense and punctuation. You might use one child's writing as a model. Encourage more able writers to extend their recounts, setting the scene and using dialogue, for example.

● Ask children to find examples of the *ar* phoneme from their own reading. Use them for spelling and handwriting practice for the week. More able children could investigate other ways of spelling the *ar* phoneme (*last*, *laugh*).

● Children can draw pictures of Mark at different points of the story and use speech bubbles to show how he feels. Alternatively, they could work in a group to consider Mark's feelings and describe them orally, or through role-play, rather than in writing.

Extension/further reading

Other Margaret Mahy stories make use of familiar themes and settings, for example *The Chewing Gum Rescue* (Methuen) and *The Great White Man-Eating Shark* (Picture Puffins). Stories about birthdays include *Gilbert and the Birthday Cake* by Jack Harvey (Hutchinson) and *Kipper's Birthday* by Mick Inkpen (Hodder). Jean Adamson's *Topsy and Tim* series (Ladybird) explores common childhood experiences.

2: 1: T5: to identify and discuss reasons for events in stories, linked to plot

2: 1: T6: to discuss familiar story themes and link to own experiences, e.g. illness, getting lost, going away

suggests his feelings

track Mark's feelings:

1. doesn't really care (too ill)

2. fed up (feeling better)

3. puzzled perhaps

4. pleased

5. excited, happy

note that feelings are not explicitly stated but implied through narrative and dialogue

emphasis

who might Sarah be? (sister)

why is he spotty?

good motive!

suggests his feelings

why? perhaps Mum knows there is unhealthy party food later

strange behaviour (because he's going to a party)

a nickname, to identify this Peter rather than another

Mum 'playing it cool'

capitals for emphasis, hyphen because not a real word

they are all ill, all have measles already

The Rare Spotted Birthday Party

1 "I feel a bit sick," said Mark. "Even if I could have a birthday, I don't think I would want it."

"That's the worst thing," said Sarah. "Not even *wanting* a birthday is worst of all."

Two days later, when the birthday really came, Mark did not feel sick any more. He just felt spotty.

He opened his presents at breakfast.

His mother and father had given him a camera. It was small, but it would take real pictures. Sarah gave him a paint box. (She always gave him a paint box. Whenever Mark got a new paint box, he gave Sarah the old one.)

All morning they painted.

2 "It feels funny today," said Mark. "It doesn't feel like a birthday. It doesn't feel special at all."

Sarah had painted a class of children. Now she began to paint spots on them.

Lunch was plain and healthy.

In the afternoon Mark's mother started to brush him all over.

3 She brushed his hair. She brushed his dressing gown, though it was new and didn't need brushing. She brushed his slippers.

"We will have a birthday drive," she said. "The car windows will stop the measles from getting out."

They drove out into the country and up a hill that Mark knew. "There's Peter's house," he said. "Peter-up-the-hill! He has measles, too."

4 "We might pay him a visit for a moment," Mark's mother said. "He won't catch measles from you if he has them already."

5 The front door was open. They rang the bell and walked in. Then Mark got a real surprise! The room was full of people. Lots of the people were boys wearing dressing-gowns – all of them spotty boys, MEASLE-Y boys.

"Happy birthday! Happy birthday!" they shouted.

2: 1: T10: to use story structure to write about own experience in same/similar form

2: 1: W3: the common spelling patterns for the vowel phonemes: *'oo'* (short as in good), *'ar'*, *'oy'* *'ow'* (Appendix List 3):
● to identify the phonemes in speech and writing
● to blend the phonemes for reading
● to segment the words into phonemes for spelling

2: 1: S4: to re-read own writing for sense and punctuation

The Magic Finger

by Roald Dahl

 P

113

Background

The Magic Finger tells the story of an eight-year-old girl (never named) who discovers that, when she gets cross, she has magic in the forefinger of her right hand. When she points it at someone who has made her cross, anything might happen to them! The story is told in the first person, which allows us to explore this point of view. The narrator addresses the reader directly several times, using a conversational style which highlights the differences between an oral retelling (as third-person narrator) and the text.

Shared reading and discussing the text

● Read the text aloud to the children, and discuss times when they have been cross and what they do when they feel like this.
● Consider why Mrs Winter became a cat, rather than anything else.
● What would the children do with a Magic Finger? Think about appropriate transformations for parents who have upset or annoyed them.
● Discuss who is telling the story. Encourage children to use the clues in the text to give information about the narrator.
● Ask the children to retell the story to each other in pairs, and then ask some to retell to the whole class. Draw out the difference between the oral retelling and the text – identifying the difference between a third-person telling and the first person – the use of *she*, rather than *I*, for example. Write out part (or all) of the retelling and identify parts where the language differs from the original. Look particularly for features of 'story language' in the original, which are likely to be missing from the retelling – such as *poor old Mrs Winter, good and strong, Guess what?*
● Track the sequence of events: the girl was unable to spell *cat* – she was sent to the corner – she was cross – she pointed the Magic Finger – Mrs Winter turned into a cat.
● Highlight words and phrases that link sentences, and identify the time and order of events – *one day, then, almost at once.*

Activities

● Look at the opening sentences of the text and note that this particular story happened some time ago (*for months…*). Note the implication that the Magic Finger is going to be used again. Consider why the girl might have used the Magic Finger before. In shared writing, model a 'prequel' to this extract – using some of the phrases from the text as a frame – *One day… Then I got cross… and almost at once… Guess what?* Demonstrate the use of the language of time to sequence and structure the writing. Model the use of capital letters for names, including the Magic Finger as the name of the special finger.
● Ask the children to make plans for their own Magic Finger stories, using the sequence identified above: something happens – get in trouble – get cross – point finger – transformation. Children can then write their own stories, in the first person, using their plans and the model from shared writing. Less able children can make a storyboard instead, showing a sequence of events, or use a writing frame. More able children might draw on features of the story language of the text, such as the conversational style as the narrator addresses the reader directly. These children might also consider the consequences of transformations, first exploring the possible outcome for Mrs Winter.

Extension/further reading

Consider the moral implications of having the power to transform people. Explore how such magic might be used for positive purposes. Make links to work in PSHE and citizenship – discuss feelings of anger, revenge and so on. If the whole text is available, discuss the moral of the story – 'putting yourself in other people's shoes'. *Matilda* by Roald Dahl (Puffin) also explores the theme of children with magic powers over adults. Children's books by James Herriot, such as *Only One Woof* and *Moses the Kitten* (both Macmillan), are told in the first person.

2: 1: T3: to be aware of the difference between spoken and written language through comparing oral recounts with text; make use of formal story elements in retelling

2: 1: T4: to understand time and sequential relationships in stories, i.e. what happened when

suggests significant previous events

traditional opening

tracking sequence:

1. incorrect spelling

2. told off

3. gets angry

4. points the finger

5. turns into a cat

6. consequences

1st person narrator; who is it? (no name)

tells us narrator is a girl

metaphor: connotations of anger/heat

informal language

time connective

addressing reader directly, like a conversation

linking phrases

again, direct address to reader

THE MAGIC FINGER

For months I had been telling myself that I would never put the Magic Finger upon anyone again – not after what happened to my teacher, old Mrs Winter.

Poor old Mrs Winter.

One day we were in class, and she was teaching us spelling. "Stand up," she said to me, "and spell cat."

1   "That's an easy one," I said. "*K-a-t.*"

2   "You are a stupid little girl!" Mrs Winter said.

"I am not a stupid little girl!" I cried. "I am a very nice little girl!"

"Go and stand in the corner," Mrs Winter said.

3   Then I got cross, and I saw red, and I put the Magic
4 Finger on Mrs Winter good and strong, and almost at once…

Guess what?

5   *Whiskers* began growing out of her face! They were long black whiskers, just like the ones you see on a cat, only much bigger. And how fast they grew! Before we had time to think, they were out to her ears!

Of course the whole class started screaming with laughter, and then Mrs Winter said, "Will you be so kind as to tell me what you find so madly funny, all of you?"

And when she turned around to write something on the blackboard we saw that she had grown a *tail* as well! It was a huge bushy tail!

I cannot begin to tell you what happened after that,
6 but if any of you are wondering whether Mrs Winter is quite all right again now, the answer is No. And she never will be.

suggests Mrs Winter may have stayed as a cat or retained feline features, or her behaviour was changed for better or worse (in the complete text, true repentance is needed in order to return to normal; perhaps Mrs Winter was not sorry about her behaviour)

2: 1: T10: to use story structure to write about own experience in same/similar form

2: 1: S2: to find examples, in fiction and non-fiction, of words and phrases that link sentences, e.g. *after, meanwhile, during, before, then, next, after a while*

2: 1: S5: to revise knowledge about other uses of capitalisation, e.g. for names, headings, titles, emphasis, and begin to use in own writing

The Werepuppy

by Jacqueline Wilson

Background

This extract is from *The Werepupppy on Holiday,* the second of Jacqueline Wilson's books about Micky and his puppy, Wolfie. Micky chooses Wolfie, a wild, seemingly untameable puppy, from the animal shelter. Micky is devoted to his pet (who he believes is a baby werewolf because of his behaviour when there is a full moon), but Micky's mum, dad and four sisters have very mixed feelings. In this extract, it is the last day of term. The other children in the class are all looking forward to exciting holidays, but Micky's family cannot afford to go away because Dad is in danger of being made redundant. Children will enjoy the humour of the text, and many will be familiar with the responsibilities of keeping a pet.

Shared reading and discussing the text

● Set the scene for the children. Read the title and consider the characteristics of a *werepuppy.*
● Read the text with the children, stopping at *Doc Martens.* Ask the children to predict what will happen.
● Read the rest of the text. Ask the children how they feel about Wolfie's behaviour towards Darren and towards Miss Monk. Draw out the fact that Wolfie seems to know how Micky feels about each of them.
● Read the first two lines again. Ask the children to discuss Micky's feelings about Wolfie. Why might Micky's plans to train Wolfie be unreasonably optimistic?
● Now read the next paragraph and ask pairs of children to describe Wolfie's character to each other. Note particularly the suggestion of a gentler side to Wolfie's nature. Why is Wolfie not so gentle with Marigold (Micky's younger sister)? (Children might want to discuss their own relationships with siblings.)
● Highlight the phrases *his teeth bared in a great grin* and *as if he was snorting with laughter.* Do dogs really grin or laugh? Consider the implied suggestion of Wolfie having almost human characteristics.

● Develop awareness of commas, exclamation marks and dialogue, when reading aloud with appropriate expression.

Activities

● Ask the children to retell the story to each other in pairs. Share ideas and write a retelling on the board. Compare this with the original. Give 'time out' with partners again to note ways in which the retelling differs. Draw out features such as description and dialogue. Discuss the differences between telling someone what happens in a story and the text itself.
● Brainstorm suggestions for a new adventure for Wolfie. Make a planning frame to include setting, characters, events and consequences. Demonstrate the use of a storyboard, using pictures to sequence events of the story and speech bubbles for dialogue.
● Children can now plan their own stories using the frame, and then compose their own storyboards. Provide less able children with partly prepared frames. Encourage more able children to add narrative and description and be adventurous with vocabulary.
● Ask children to make a 'Wanted' poster for Wolfie, describing him and his 'crimes'.

Extension/further reading

Children can consider what might happen with Wolfie on the holiday or on a night with a full moon. If the book is available, ask the children how each character feels about Wolfie. Children with pets can write descriptions of them. Children without pets could write about one they would like to have. Make PSHE and citizenship links to the responsibilities involved in keeping a pet. *Mark Spark in the Dark* (Puffin) is another Jacqueline Wilson book suitable for young readers. Stories and poems about pets include *Be Gentle* by Virginia Miller (Walker Books), *No Worries!* by Marcia Williams (Walker Books), *Pet Poems* compiled by John Foster (OUP), *The Harry Hamster Hunt,* compiled by Tony Bradman (MacDonald Young).

2: 1: S3: to recognise and take account of commas and exclamation marks in reading aloud with appropriate expression

2: 1: S6: to use a variety of simple organisational devices, e.g. arrows, lines, boxes, keys, to indicate sequences and relationships

The Werepuppy

"I'm going to have a smashing summer, Miss Monk," said Micky. "I'm going to take Wolfie to the park every day."

The last time Micky had taken him to the park, Wolfie had picked a fight with every dog in sight, barked hysterically at the ducks on the pond, and snatched an ice-cream from a small child's hand and swallowed it in one gulp. The ice-cream, not the hand. Wolfie was actually quite gentle with most little children. Apart from Marigold.

"I'm going to spend the summer getting Wolfie to obey all my orders," said Micky, with unreasonable optimism.

Mum brought Wolfie with her when she came to meet Micky and Marigold when school broke up. Wolfie came flying across the playground, his teeth bared in a great grin, his grey fur sticking up spikily.

Most of the children laughed and pointed. Some stepped back rather rapidly out of Wolfie's way. Darren Smith just happened to be bending down, doing up his Doc Martens. Wolfie spotted him and his grin grew wider. He decided to try out a goat imitation. He lowered his head and charged. Wolfie butted Darren right on the bottom and sent him flying.

Darren wasn't hurt. Just his dignity. Everyone laughed at him. Micky practically fell about, and Wolfie gave short sharp barks as if he was snorting with laughter too.

Darren didn't find it funny at all.

"That mangy old dog ought to be put down!" he yelled. "You keep it away from me, Micky."

"I think it's certainly about time you got your dog trained, Micky," said Miss Monk, crossing the playground.

"He can be quite good sometimes, honestly, Miss," said Micky.

And as if to prove his point Wolfie wiped his paws on the sprawling Darren Smith and trotted meekly up to Miss Monk, head a little bowed, as if overcome by her presence.

Annotations (left margin):
- shows Micky's devotion to Wolfie
- commas aid reading
- Mickey's younger sister; Wolfie's attitude towards her is revealing about Micky and Marigold's relationship
- easy to predict what will happen
- what do goats do?
- short phrases for effect

Annotations (right margin):
- Micky's teacher
- humour; authentic of child narrator
- why is it unreasonable?
- almost human description; it may be a grin, but there are lots of teeth
- pride
- again, human qualities
- shows Darren's feelings – hurt, angry, embarrassed

Annotations (bottom):
- quite restrained reaction from a teacher; revealing about her feelings towards Micky and Darren
- again, suggests human qualities – Wolfie seems to be aware of who Micky likes and who he doesn't

2: 1: T3: to be aware of the difference between spoken and written language through comparing oral recounts with text; make use of formal story elements in retelling;

2: 1: T5: to identify and discuss reasons for events in stories, linked to plot

I'm not scared of the monster by John Foster

Background

This poem explores a common childhood fear – of what might be beneath the bed or behind the door at night. The repeated *I'm not scared* is a familiar boast, used by children to make themselves seem brave even if they do not feel it. The poem has a regular verse structure and rhyme and rhythm patterns within each verse, making it ideal for learning and reciting aloud. The rhymes do not always share the same rime, allowing exploration of words with similar sounds but different spellings.

Shared reading and discussing the text

● Conceal the title of the poem (and possibly the last word of each verse) and read the poem with the children, encouraging them to supply the missing words. Ask them to suggest what the title might be – discuss this in pairs and share ideas before revealing the title.

● Ask the children whether they think there really are monsters in the bedroom and whether the child in the poem is scared or not. Draw out the fact that the repetition of *I'm not scared* and the head-patting and paw-shaking might be acts of bravado.

● Discuss the children's experiences of being frightened – particularly at night-time. Make links to PSHE and citizenship, exploring fears.

● Consider how the children knew what the missing words were in the initial reading, drawing attention to the rhymes. Read the text again and highlight rhyming words. Note rhymes that share a rime and those which do not. Emphasise that although words may sound the same they do not always look the same.

● Look at the layout of the poem and encourage the children to describe the structure, using appropriate terminology such as *verse* and *line*. Note the five-line verse pattern, the repeated lines and the rhyme pattern. Read aloud again, emphasising the rhythms. (You could draw attention to *'cause* in the last verse – abbreviated to preserve the rhythm, and also perhaps to suggest the child's voice.)

● Read aloud again, asking the children to focus on punctuation – note how lines flow where there is no punctuation at the end of each one. Note capitals at the beginning of each line (even if it is not a new sentence).

● Look closely at the vocabulary variations within verses 1 to 3, particularly the effect of the words describing the monster's presence – *hides*, *lurks*, *skulks*. Monsters conceal themselves in order to scare! Also note *pat*, *shake*, *stroke* – what you might do to a pet!

● Focus on the last verse and highlight the differences. Consider the satisfactory concluding effect of this final verse.

Activities

● Pairs can brainstorm additions to the rhymes in the poem, generating rhyming families. Children may work in mixed-ability pairs to explore the spellings of rhyming words. More able children could use dictionaries to sort words into rime groups.

● Children can learn and perform the poem, paying attention to rhythms, punctuation and expression – perhaps in groups of four, taking one verse each, or in groups of three, taking a couplet each plus the last line of each verse. Actions could be added. Encourage the children to evaluate their own and others' performances of the poem, focusing on the rhythms and expression and taking account of punctuation.

Extension/further reading

Use shared writing to create a class poem for an anthology, adopting the same structure. The children could use ICT to present the poem, taking advantage of facilities such as clip art. Other poems that explore fear of the dark and night-time include 'The Dark' by Adrian Henri (*The Puffin Book of Fantastic First Poems*), 'In the Middle of the Night' by John Foster (*Bare Bear and other rhymes* (OUP) and 'Bedtime' by Allan Ahlberg (*The Puffin Book of Utterly Brilliant Poetry*). Stories that also explore this theme include *What on Earth was That?* by Paul Geraghty (Hodder).

2: 1: T7: to learn, re-read and recite favourite poems, taking account of punctuation; to comment on aspects such as word combinations, sound patterns (such as rhymes, rhythms, alliterative patterns) and forms of presentation

repeated phrase – gives structure to poem and emphasises child's attempts to convince himself/ herself

ABCCB rhyming pattern

I'm not scared of the monster

I'm not scared of the monster A
That hides beneath my bed. B
When it leaps out C
To prowl about, C
I pat it on the head. B

I'm not scared of the monster
That lurks behind the door.
When it leaps out
To prowl about,
I shake its furry paw.

I'm not scared of the monster
That skulks under the chair.
When it leaps out
To prowl about,
I stroke its spiky hair.

I'm not scared of the monsters,
'Cause they're no longer there.
When I leapt out
To scream and shout,
I gave them all a scare!

John Foster

powerful verbs to describe monster's creepy actions

child's 'actions' to imaginary monster may be acts of bravado

capital letter at beginning of each line, even when not a new sentence

plural; contrast in last verse

abbreviation to preserve rhythm (and reflect child's voice)

change in last verse – similar structure but different emphasis: monsters have been scared away by child

past tense – monsters are gone

provides closure for poem, and child can now go to sleep

2: 1: T8: to collect and categorise poems to build class anthologies

2: 1: S5: to revise knowledge about other uses of capitalisation, e.g. for names, headings, titles, emphasis, and begin to use in own writing

2: 1: W4: to investigate and classify words with the same sounds but different spellings

Don't

by John Kitching

Background

Children will be familiar with adults (in this case, parents) telling them not to do certain things. This poem is told from the child's point of view, but using the adult's voice (or child's imitation of it!) throughout most of it. It is a list poem, using the repeated *Don't* as the opening for each line. The repetition gives the child's perspective – that all adults ever say to them is *'Don't'*. The rhyming pattern is mostly at the ends of alternate lines and offers some opportunity for exploring words that rhyme but do not share a rime. The different voices in the poem present the opportunity for 'performance'. List poems provide children with a simple structure for writing their own poems.

Shared reading and discussing the text

● First, discuss the title, considering what the poem might be about and who might be speaking.

● Now read the poem aloud with the children, using appropriate voices. Discuss whose point of view this presents.

● In pairs, ask the children to discuss their own experiences of adults saying *'Don't'* and feed these back to the class. Consider why adults say *'Don't'* to children. Focus on some of the *Don'ts* from the poem and suggest reasons why these things are frowned upon by adults (for example, cruelty to animals, bad manners/impoliteness). Ask children whether they think they are reasonable *Don'ts*. (You might also ask them to rephrase the lines as *Dos*, such as *Do treat the cat kindly, Do use a handkerchief…* and consider the effect of the change.)

● Re-read the poem, with groups or individuals taking different lines and with a choral rendering of the last two lines.

● Focus on the layout and structure of the poem. Consider the repetition of *Don't*, which emphasises the child's point of view that adults are always saying *'Don't'*. Note that each line (except the first and last two) is a short complete sentence, which makes the voice sound insistent and 'bossy'. The first line is, in effect, two lines in one and sums up the poem – you can't do anything! The last two lines are separated to highlight the new voice, with a pause and italic for emphasis.

● Ask the children to find and highlight the rhyming words and note the different spellings in places – *thumb/gum, me/tea, glue/do*.

Activities

● Ask the children to brainstorm the kinds of *Don'ts* that teachers say and use these in shared writing to begin a new poem. Keep the focus on the ideas, the repetition and the short, clipped sentences.

● Children can use the poem begun in shared writing to write their own *Don't* list poems (or in pairs) – perhaps choosing a different adult (lunchtime supervisors, older brothers or sisters, for example) or a situation (in the playground, out visiting). More able children might be able to make their poems rhyme without losing the structure and effect. The poems can then be illustrated and collected into a class book.

● Ask the children to find additional rhyming words for those in the poem and to investigate their spellings.

Extension/further reading

Write *Do* poems (*Do tidy your room, Do hurry up…*). Write subversive versions, suggesting what life might be like if children were allowed to do whatever they wished (*Do run in the corridor, Do slide down the banisters…*). The children can perform their poems with actions. 'Don't' by Richard Edwards, available in *Read a Poem, Write a Poem* (Simon and Schuster), is a similar list poem. Other list poems include 'Two Lists' by Tony Bradman (also available in *Read a Poem, Write a Poem*), 'The Teacher's Day in Bed' by David Orme in *The Works* edited by Paul Cookson (MacMillan), 'Things I have been doing lately' by Allan Ahlberg in *The Puffin Book of Utterly Brilliant Poetry*. 'Things I'd do if it wasn't for Mum' by Tony Mitton (in *The Works*) incorporates a similar theme.

2: 1: T7: to learn, re-read and recite favourite poems, taking account of punctuation; to comment on aspects such as word combinations, sound patterns (such as rhymes, rhythms, alliterative patterns) and forms of presentation

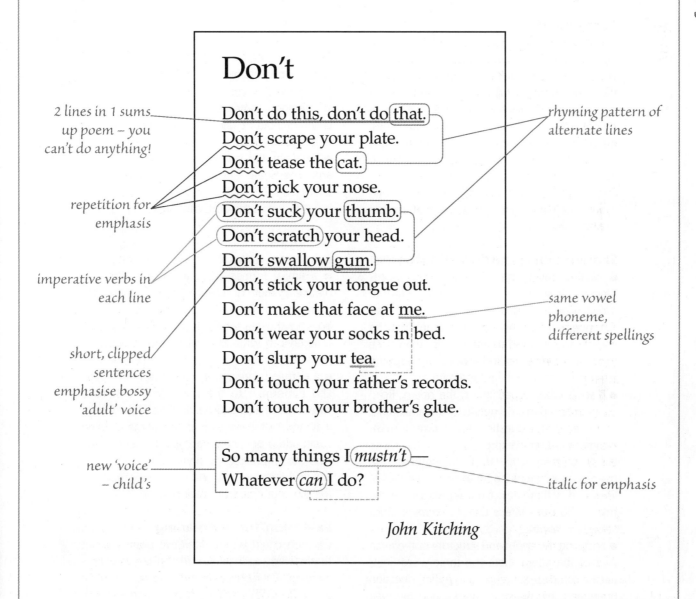

Don't

Don't do this, don't do that.
Don't scrape your plate.
Don't tease the cat.
Don't pick your nose.
Don't suck your thumb.
Don't scratch your head.
Don't swallow gum.
Don't stick your tongue out.
Don't make that face at me.
Don't wear your socks in bed.
Don't slurp your tea.
Don't touch your father's records.
Don't touch your brother's glue.

So many things I *mustn't* —
Whatever *can* I do?

John Kitching

Annotations:

2 lines in 1 sums up poem – you can't do anything!

repetition for emphasis

imperative verbs in each line

short, clipped sentences emphasise bossy 'adult' voice

new 'voice' – child's

rhyming pattern of alternate lines

same vowel phoneme, different spellings

italic for emphasis

2: 1: T8: to collect and categorise poems to build class anthologies

2: 1: T12: to use simple poetry structures and to substitute own ideas, write new lines

2: 1: W4: to investigate and classify words with the same sounds but different spellings

Dinner-time Rhyme

by June Crebbin

Background

This is a poem in two voices – dinner lady and children – in the form of questions and answers. The structure is regular and simple. The basis of the poem is the rhyming connection between the children's names and food. The rhymes are found both at the ends of lines and within lines, making reading aloud an opportunity to enjoy the sound patterns. The first three lines are an introduction to the content and form. The last three lines form a humorous conclusion and suggest defeat on the part of the poet, unable to find a rhyme.

Shared reading and discussing the text

● Initially, cover the rhyming food words (perhaps leaving the first two uncovered to allow children to discover the pattern) and read the poem, with the children supplying the missing words. Read together more than once to enjoy the rhythms and rhymes. Try clapping a regular beat to highlight the rhythm.

● Discuss who is speaking in the poem. Read again in two parts – dinner lady and children – to appreciate the question-and-answer format, paying attention to expression.

● Ask pairs of children to identify all the rhyming words, looking for those at the ends of lines and within lines. Note words where the rhymes do not share a rime (*Pete/meat, Sue/stew, Pam/lamb*).

● Focus on the layout and structure of the main part of the poem. Note the three-word lines, each a complete sentence, alternating question (identified by question mark) and answer. Notice how the author has indented the reply each time to highlight the couplets.

● Look at the first two and last three lines, which do not conform to the rest of the poem's pattern. Consider the poet's reasons for these differences – an introduction or scene setting, and a conclusion. Note that the phrase from the first line is almost repeated, making a link and rounding off the poem. The poet admits defeat on a rhyme for *Katerina Wilhelmina…* Emphasise the pause before the final line (as the poet tries to find a rhyme). Perhaps her name could be shortened to find a rhyme (like Sam, Sue, Greg …) – *Kat likes fat.*

● It may be possible to find rhymes for some of the names of children in your class (again, shortening names may help). More able children could be given rhyming dictionaries to find rhymes for their own name.

● Highlight the *ow* phoneme in *How ab<u>ou</u>t,* and investigate and categorise other words containing the same phoneme, noting that *ou* is not found at the ends of words.

Activities

● In shared writing, begin an alliteration poem, in a similar format, using initial letters/sounds of the names of children in the class, for example *Paul likes pizza, Leanne likes lollies.*

● Using the starter from shared writing, the children can write class alliteration poems, in pairs or individually.

● Ask the children to learn the poem in pairs and perform it to the class (or in assembly, where half the class takes the role of the dinner lady and half are the children). Some children could add a percussion accompaniment to the poem to emphasise the rhythm.

● Ask the children to find further examples of the *ow* phoneme from their reading.

Extension/further reading

Children could write alliterative poems about themselves – such as *Paul likes pizza, Paul likes painting, Paul likes presents* and so on. Read and collect other school, food or name poems for a class anthology, for example 'An Alphabet of Horrible Habits' by Colin West (a name poem, using a name for each letter of the alphabet), available in *Twinkle Twinkle Chocolate Bar* compiled by John Foster (OUP). Allan Ahlberg has written two collections of school poems: *Please Mrs Butler* and *Heard it in the Playground* (both Puffin). Food poems can be found in *The Puffin Book of Fantastic First Poems*, Brian Patten's *Gargling with Jelly* (Puffin) and *Twinkle Twinkle Chocolate Bar.*

2: 1: T7: to learn, re-read and recite favourite poems, taking account of punctuation; to comment on aspects such as word combinations, sound patterns (such as rhymes, rhythms, alliterative patterns) and forms of presentation

2: 1: T8: to collect and categorise poems to build class anthologies

2: 1: T12: to use simple poetry structures and to substitute own ideas, write new lines

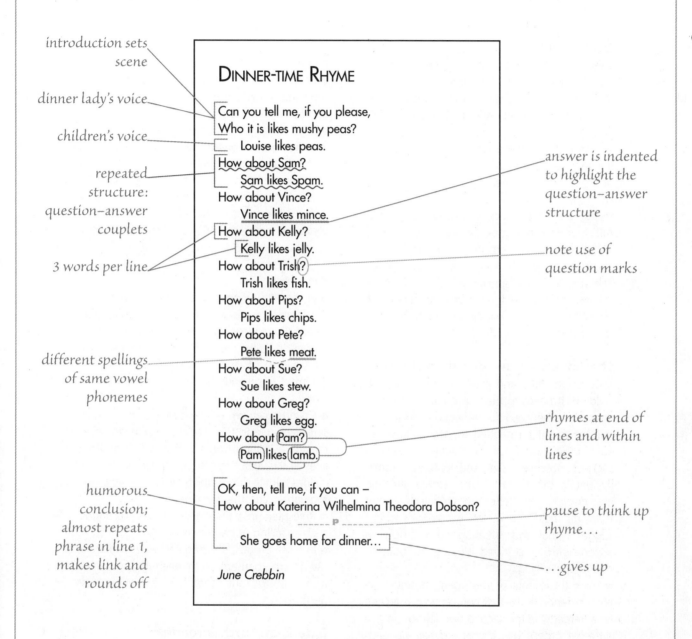

introduction sets scene

dinner lady's voice

children's voice

repeated structure: question–answer couplets

3 words per line

different spellings of same vowel phonemes

humorous conclusion; almost repeats phrase in line 1, makes link and rounds off

DINNER-TIME RHYME

Can you tell me, if you please,
Who it is likes mushy peas?
    Louise likes peas.
How about Sam?
    Sam likes Spam.
How about Vince?
    Vince likes mince.
How about Kelly?
    Kelly likes jelly.
How about Trish?
    Trish likes fish.
How about Pips?
    Pips likes chips.
How about Pete?
    Pete likes meat.
How about Sue?
    Sue likes stew.
How about Greg?
    Greg likes egg.
How about Pam?
    Pam likes lamb.

OK, then, tell me, if you can –
How about Katerina Wilhelmina Theodora Dobson?
- - - - - P - - - - -
    She goes home for dinner...

June Crebbin

answer is indented to highlight the question–answer structure

note use of question marks

rhymes at end of lines and within lines

pause to think up rhyme…

…gives up

2: 1: W3: the common spelling patterns for the vowel phonemes: 'oo' (short as in *good*), 'ar', 'oy' 'ow' (Appendix List 3):
- to identify the phonemes in speech and writing
- to blend the phonemes for reading
- to segment the words into phonemes for spelling

Best Friends

by Bernard Young

Background

This is a poem about falling out and making up with friends, a theme familiar to most children. It allows them to explore the responsibilities and obligations of friendship, the good times and the bad times. The poem has a clear structure of verses and repeated phrases but no rhymes, although the patterned repetition offers a rhythmic 'feel'. It works rather like a story with a moral – falling out with a best friend and then forgiving and forgetting. Although taking a question-and-answer form, it is a monologue with only one voice asking and responding, speaking as if to him/herself. The structure and familiar subject will enable children to explore their own experiences of friendship and write their own poems in a similar form.

Shared reading and discussing the text

● Cover the title and read the poem to the children. It needs to be read quite slowly with pauses at the gaps for reflection. A second reading might be needed for the children to absorb the 'story'. Ask the children in pairs to suggest possible titles and consider some, evaluating the effect of each. Reveal the title and discuss. The generic *best friends*, rather than *my best friend* for example, perhaps suggests that this situation could apply to anyone with a best friend. It might also point to the 'happy ending'.

● Track the events of the poem, noting how each 'offence' in the first two verses is matched by a 'remedy' in the second two (although in a different order). Use a chart to pair up each offence and its remedy (which may be actions or saying *sorry*).

● Make links to PSHE and discuss the behaviour of the two characters, and the moral of the story – the apparent misunderstanding (think about how this might have arisen), the apologies and the forgiveness. Consider the feelings of the narrator (and the friend) at different stages. Ask the children to think about their own experiences of falling out with friends and their feelings at the time.

● Read the poem again, together, and consider how the reading reflects the changing mood and feelings in the poem.

● Look closely at the structure of the poem, identifying the repeated pattern of the first four verses (*Would a best friend … Mine did*). The fourth verse has an extra line – to introduce the reason for the friend's actions. Note the change of form and focus of the final verse: the earlier verses describe the friend's actions, the last verse is what 'I' did, expressed *simply*.

Activities

● In shared writing, make a plan for a poem in the same form, using a chart like that drawn up earlier. Share ideas on 'offences' and 'remedies'. Model or scribe the first verse, demonstrating the layout of the poem, highlighting the indented lines and the way *Mine did* stands alone.

● Children can write their own poems, using a similar plan, and the modelled verse structure. Provide a writing frame with the first and last lines of the verses for less able children. Put the children into mixed-ability pairs to edit and evaluate each other's poems.

● Role-play, in pairs, 'best friends' scenarios, such as falling out and making up.

● In small groups, children can learn and recite the poem, perhaps with each group taking a verse to put together a whole-class performance.

Extension/further reading

Turn the poem into a first-person narrative piece of prose, beginning with the possible cause of the misunderstanding *I thought you'd fallen out with me*. Compile a class book of the children's poems. Allan Ahlberg has written several poems about friends, such as 'It is a puzzle', 'Small quarrel' and 'Is that your apple?', all available in his collection *Please Mrs Butler* (Puffin).

2: 1: **T6:** to discuss familiar story themes and link to own experiences, e.g. illness, getting lost, going away

2: 1: **T7:** to learn, re-read and recite favourite poems, taking account of punctuation; to comment on aspects such as word combinations, sound patterns (such as rhymes, rhythms, alliterative patterns) and forms of presentation

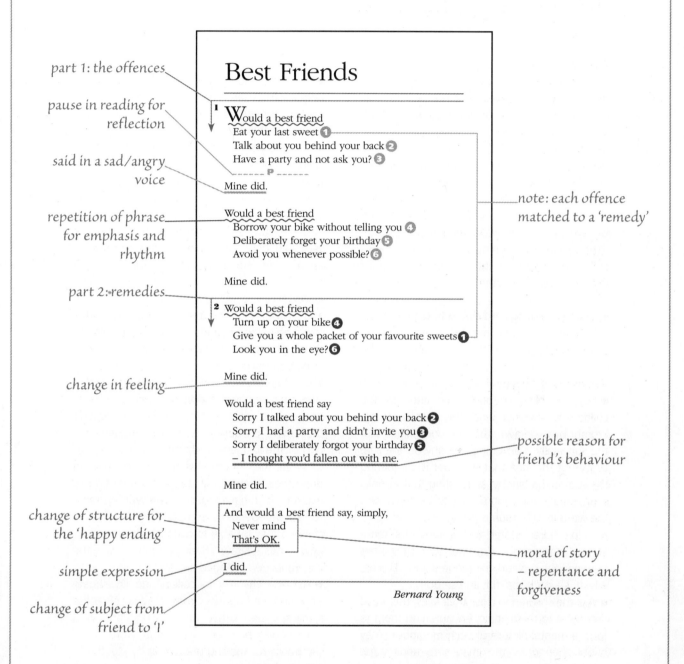

part 1: the offences

pause in reading for reflection

said in a sad/angry voice

repetition of phrase for emphasis and rhythm

part 2: remedies

change in feeling

change of structure for the 'happy ending'

simple expression

change of subject from friend to 'I'

note: each offence matched to a 'remedy'

possible reason for friend's behaviour

moral of story – repentance and forgiveness

Best Friends

1 Would a best friend
  Eat your last sweet **1**
  Talk about you behind your back **2**
  Have a party and not ask you? **3**
------ P ------
Mine did.

Would a best friend
  Borrow your bike without telling you **4**
  Deliberately forget your birthday **5**
  Avoid you whenever possible? **6**

Mine did.

2 Would a best friend
  Turn up on your bike **4**
  Give you a whole packet of your favourite sweets **1**
  Look you in the eye? **6**

Mine did.

Would a best friend say
  Sorry I talked about you behind your back **2**
  Sorry I had a party and didn't invite you **3**
  Sorry I deliberately forgot your birthday **5**
  – I thought you'd fallen out with me.

Mine did.

And would a best friend say, simply,
  Never mind
  That's OK.

I did.

Bernard Young

2: 1: **T12:** to use simple poetry structures and to substitute own ideas, write new lines

2: 1: **S6:** to use a variety of simple organisational devices, e.g. arrows, lines, boxes, keys, to indicate sequences and relationships

What is the sun? by Wes Magee

Background

This poem introduces children to the figurative use of language, explored through a familiar object, drawing two-line 'word pictures' of the sun. The structure is simple as each image is a couplet, where the first line introduces the colour and shape of the sun by way of metaphor and the second extends the metaphor into the sky, suggesting how the object got there and what it is doing. The format will allow children to develop their powers of imagination through their own writing, enjoying the visual images created by words, without the constraints of rhymes or regular rhythms.

Shared reading and discussing the text

● Read the title and then the poem with the children, noting how the poem answers the question in the title. Identify and discuss any unfamiliar vocabulary.

● Read the first couplet again and ask the children to consider what the poet is saying. Prompt by asking whether the poet thinks that the sun really is an orange dinghy on the sea. Draw out the idea that the poet is comparing the sun to the dinghy, suggesting that it looks similar, and comparing the sky to the sea. Insert the word *like* (*The sun is like an orange dinghy*) to help children appreciate the non-literal sense of the description. Consider the similarities between the sun and an orange dinghy. Discuss why it is a *calm* sea (flat and smooth).

● Ask the children to close their eyes, then read the poem to them again, encouraging them to form a mental picture of each metaphor. They might then draw the images to understand how the poet uses words to 'paint a picture'.

● Pick out and list each image of the sun, looking at the range of colours and shapes. Repeat for the sky images. Note that the second verse does not refer directly to the sky; this metaphor may need further discussion.

● Highlight the verbs, noting how these extend the metaphor, and focus on the *-ing* and *-ed* endings, practising the spelling of each suffix.

Activities

● Brainstorm ideas for a class composition. Begin with round or spherical objects (*ball, orange, wheel*), and then add the different colours of the sun. Take one of the images and model the writing of a new line for the poem. Now demonstrate how to extend the image by brainstorming colours (*indigo, turquoise, bluebell,* or colours other than blue) and objects (*glass, plate, carpet*) for the sky. Note how the two lines flow as a single sentence by adding a verb and draw attention to *-ing* and *-ed* as appropriate. For example, *the sun is a ripe orange waiting on a bright blue plate.* Share ideas for a second new line, select an image, and scribe this. Discuss how this new idea might be extended and ask children, in pairs, to continue the new image into the next line, using your model.

● Children should now be able to write further lines to continue the poem, working in pairs, using ideas generated by the class or adding their own. Encourage them to consider each part of the image first, then put them together to write their lines. Less able children could draw their images first. Use guided writing to extend the initial images, and a writing frame to aid independent composition. More able children may be able to use alliteration in their new lines. Draw their attention to the alliteration Wes Magee has used.

● Ask the children to collect and investigate *-ing* and *-ed* words from reading. Practise spelling the suffix in conjunction with handwriting practice. Use colour words from the poem for spelling practice and extend it to other colours.

Extension/further reading

More able children could write poems about the moon in a similar format. Children can share their favourite lines from their own compositions, stating why they particularly liked them. Ask other children to comment on the effectiveness of the imagery.

2: 1: **T7:** to learn, re-read and recite favourite poems, taking account of punctuation; to comment on aspects such as word combinations, sound patterns (such as rhymes, rhythms, alliterative patterns) and forms of presentation

2: 1: **T8:** to collect and categorise poems to build class anthologies

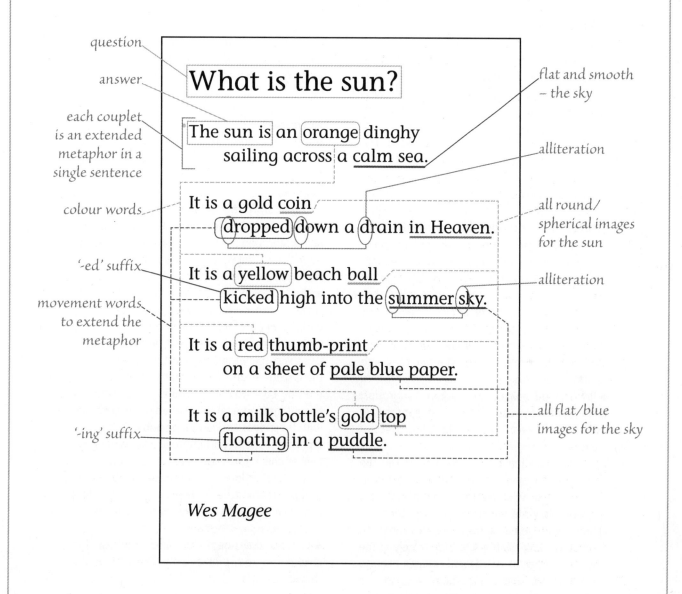

question

answer

each couplet is an extended metaphor in a single sentence

colour words

'-ed' suffix

movement words to extend the metaphor

'-ing' suffix

flat and smooth – the sky

alliteration

all round/ spherical images for the sun

alliteration

all flat/blue images for the sky

What is the sun?

The sun is an orange dinghy
  sailing across a calm sea.

It is a gold coin
  dropped down a drain in Heaven.

It is a yellow beach ball
  kicked high into the summer sky.

It is a red thumb-print
  on a sheet of pale blue paper.

It is a milk bottle's gold top
  floating in a puddle.

Wes Magee

2: 1: **T12:** to use simple poetry structures and to substitute own ideas, write new lines

2: 1: **W7:** to use word endings, e.g. 's' (plural), 'ed' (past tense), 'ing' (present tense) to support their reading and spelling

2: 1: **W9:** to spell common irregular words from Appendix List 1

Dad

by Berlie Doherty

Background

This is a lively, rhythmic poem, describing Dad in different moods – energetic and playful, or sleepy and grumpy. Many children will identify with the changing moods of the people who look after them! The poem is based largely on two-word phrases, using language creatively and figuratively to develop images of Dad. The rhythms of the poem reflect the moods, and there are rhymes throughout, sometimes at the ends of lines and sometimes within them.

Shared reading and discussing the text

● Read the poem to the children, reflecting the changing moods through pace and expression. Discuss any unfamiliar vocabulary (such as *bucking bronco*). Ask the children what they learn about the dad of the poem. What do they notice about the two parts of the poem? Give them time to discuss their own dads, or any other family member, and whether they also have different moods.

● Read aloud again, the children (or groups) taking turns to read lines, using appropriate expression for each part, and taking account of commas.

● Ask the children to describe the dad in the poem in their own words (without looking at the text). Use whiteboards, divided into two sections, to write words or phrases for each mood. Write some of the children's ideas on the board. Now ask them to look closely at the poem and find the words and phrases used to describe Dad. Encourage them to find the evidence for their own descriptions (for example, 'happy' – *laughing-bear*).

● Highlight some of the hyphenated phrases and expand the images. For example, you might say that Dad is a *laughing-bear* because his laugh is loud and roaring. Ask the children to expand on other images in the same way (perhaps working in pairs, taking a phrase each). Draw attention to the figurative use of much of the language. Point out the hyphens, which join two words to create a single picture.

● Ask mixed-ability pairs to find the rhymes and highlight them, noting where they appear in the line. Draw attention to the way the poet varies both the rhyme scheme and the structure of lines.

Activities

● Ask the children to discuss in pairs some of the things their 'good mood' mums do. Model how to turn some ideas into two-word phrases (for example, *My mum reads me stories* becomes *story-reader*), and use these to write the first two or three lines of a new poem. Repeat for 'bad mood' mum. Rhymes need not be included unless they arise naturally, as this can interfere with ideas.

● Using the model from shared writing, the children can continue poems independently, working in pairs. Some children may be given a writing frame with a limited number of lines. Use the plenary to add the last two lines, noting the change from *he* to *I*, the sense of loss and the link back to the first line – *dancing-man*. Encourage more able children to experiment with their ideas and language and to work with a partner to read and improve their writing, as well as check for sense and punctuation.

● Ask the children to act out the poem in groups, reading with expression and adding actions to illustrate the images. This can lead to a whole-class performance.

● Cut up the poem into lines and ask the children to reassemble it by looking for the rhyming words.

Extension/further reading

Other family poems that will appeal to children include 'Grandpa' by Berlie Doherty, 'Our Mother' by Allan Ahlberg, 'Granny Granny Please Comb My Hair' by Grace Nichols, 'My Brother' by Theresa Heine – all available in *The Puffin Book of Fantastic First Poems*. 'My Sister's Eating Porridge' by John Coldwell and 'Undertable Land' by Paul Rogers can be found in *Twinkle Twinkle Chocolate Bar* (OUP).

part 1: happy, playful (read with pace, lively)

metaphor: his laugh is loud like a bear's

2-word pictures

Jack and the Beanstalk perhaps

DAD

1 Dad is the dancing-man
The laughing-bear, the prickle-chin,
The tickle-fingers, jungle-roars
Bucking bronco, rocking-horse,
The helicopter roundabout ᴿ
The beat-the-wind at swing-and-shout ᴿ
Goal-post, scarey-ghost ᴿ
Climbing-Jack, humpty-back. ᴿ

shaving stubble

commas give the feel of a list

rhymes

rhymes within lines

part 2: sleepy, grumpy (read more slowly, drawl)

alliteration and onomatopoeia suggest snoring

conclusion = child's response

2 But sometimes he's
A go-away-please!
A snorey-snarl, a sprawly slump
A yawny mouth, a sleeping lump,

And I'm a kite without a string
Waiting for Dad to dance again.

Berlie Doherty

no direction, unable to do anything without Dad

links back to first line of Dad as 'dancing-man'

Chewy Chocolate Crunch Cakes

Background

This simple recipe, within many children's experience, demonstrates common features of the instruction genre, in terms of layout and organisation, and the language used. It employs imperative verbs and has a title, a goal, materials and equipment needed and a set of sequenced (numbered) steps to achieve the finished product. The instructions are given concisely, in simple language, while offering the opportunity for discussion of subject-specific vocabulary. It makes cross-curricular links with science on changing materials, through the observation of melting chocolate and butter.

Shared reading and discussing the text

● Read the text and ask the children what kind of text it is. Where might it have come from? Who might use it?

● Let the children discuss and share their own experiences of recipes and cooking.

● Ask the children to consider why people use recipes. Draw out of the discussion that when we tell people how to do something we are giving *instructions*.

● Re-read the text in sections, discussing the purpose of each, and exploring unfamiliar or specialised vocabulary. Identify the title, the goal (to make 16 cakes), the ingredients (the food items needed; consider weights at a level appropriate for the class; discuss and clarify terms such as *plain, unsalted*), the equipment (the tools or utensils needed – clarify terminology as it arises; have these items on display in the classroom), and the instructions themselves (what you do with the ingredients to make the cakes). Label these features for future reference.

● Ask the children to look at presentational features (size of font, bold, capital letters, indents) and consider why they are used.

● Consider the order of the sections – put up a version of the text where the sections are reordered and consider the problems presented. (For example, you first need to gather ingredients to make sure you have everything.)

● Consider why the instructions are numbered. Could they be followed in any order?

● Play a version of 'Simon Says', where pairs of children give each other short, simple instructions such as *stand up, turn round, touch your nose*. Notice the direct language used – talking directly to the person receiving the instructions. Write some of these instructions on the board. Which are the words that say what action is required? Highlight them and draw attention to their position as the first word of each instruction.

● Re-read *What to do* and identify the words that state the action, for example *Break, Put, Heat…* Highlight these words and again note their position.

Activities

● In small groups, with assistance, the children can follow the instructions to make the cakes. Ask them to evaluate the instructions and consider what else could have been included, perhaps pictures of each stage, safety advice.

● Children can draw a sequence of pictures to demonstrate the steps in the recipe, then cut them up and ask a partner to arrange them in the correct order, using numbers or arrows to identify the correct sequence.

● Give mixed-ability pairs cut-up copies of the recipe, with numbers removed, to reassemble.

● In groups, ask children to make posters to illustrate the key features of recipes, taking the labelled text as a model.

Extension/further reading

Find examples of instructions in the classroom (perhaps on the computer or on a construction kit). Children could discuss in pairs other occasions when they might have needed or used instructions (for example, how to get somewhere, how to play a game). Make a list and encourage children to bring examples of instructional texts for display. Children may be able to follow other recipes to produce dishes (link to science and design and technology) and evaluate their effectiveness.

2: 1: **T13:** to read simple written instructions in the classroom, simple recipes, plans, instructions for constructing something

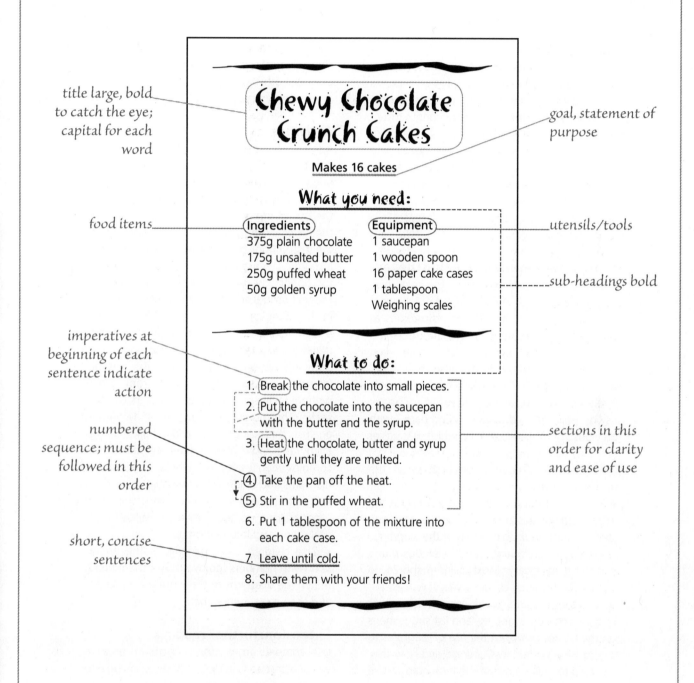

title large, bold to catch the eye; capital for each word

goal, statement of purpose

food items

utensils/tools

sub-headings bold

imperatives at beginning of each sentence indicate action

numbered sequence; must be followed in this order

sections in this order for clarity and ease of use

short, concise sentences

Chewy Chocolate Crunch Cakes

Makes 16 cakes

What you need:

Ingredients
375g plain chocolate
175g unsalted butter
250g puffed wheat
50g golden syrup

Equipment
1 saucepan
1 wooden spoon
16 paper cake cases
1 tablespoon
Weighing scales

What to do:

1. Break the chocolate into small pieces.
2. Put the chocolate into the saucepan with the butter and the syrup.
3. Heat the chocolate, butter and syrup gently until they are melted.
4. Take the pan off the heat.
5. Stir in the puffed wheat.
6. Put 1 tablespoon of the mixture into each cake case.
7. Leave until cold.
8. Share them with your friends!

2: 1: **T14:** to note key structural features, e.g. clear statement of purpose at start, sequential steps set out in a list, direct language

2: 1: **S5:** to revise knowledge about other uses of capitalisation, e.g. for names, headings, titles, emphasis, and begin to use in own writing

The concertina book by Paul Johnson

Background

This set of instructions for making a simple concertina book has many of the features commonly found in instructional texts: a title, diagrams and sequenced instructions, written in the imperative. Making books can be a valuable motivational tool for developing children's writing. A child's own book can be used across the curriculum: it gives writing real purpose and audience and also provides a helpful structure. This text is, therefore, set in a sound classroom context.

Shared reading and discussing the text

● Before showing the children the text, give each child (or each pair) a piece of A4 paper and ask them to carry out the instructions as you read them. Compare finished products. It is likely that some children will have been unsuccessful; discuss the difficulties.

● Now give out copies of the diagrams only (without the text), and ask them to try again, using only the diagrams. Compare with previous attempts and discuss which was easier and why. It is likely that some children will still have been unsuccessful; establish what the difficulties were.

● Now reveal the complete text. Carry out the activity again, this time reading the text one step at a time, looking carefully at the diagrams, discussing vocabulary, and demonstrating yourself if necessary. Most children should be successful this time; consider why it was easier.

● Ask the children to discuss what makes instructions easy to follow, and list suggestions on the board. Draw out the use of diagrams to support the written instructions, and how they can help to make sense of the terminology. Use arrows or cut-up versions of the text to demonstrate how each diagram corresponds to one step in the written instructions, noting the corresponding numbers.

● Highlight the words in the text that indicate the action to be taken – *Lay, Fold...* Note that in most cases this comes at the beginning of each line. Focus on instructions 3 and 5, noting *Then*

and *Now* and how they emphasise the chronological sequence of the instructions. Consider other words that might be used, and insert them into the text.

Activities

● In a shared writing session, give some construction bricks to one pair of children. Ask one child to give the other a short sequence of instructions to build a simple shape. Encourage the use of imperatives and words that identify the order – *First... Next...* Demonstrate writing the instructions on the board, using the text as a model. Discuss how to incorporate diagrams to support the written instructions. Annotate the text produced – title, diagrams, instructions in chronological order, 'time' words.

● Provide pairs of children with construction materials to build simple shapes, giving each other instructions. They can then write out their instructions, using the model from shared writing, including diagrams. The pairs can help each other check features of their writing against those identified and labelled earlier. Encourage more able children to make more complex constructions, where precision of diagrams and language is essential.

● Children could swap their instructions with other children to see if they can follow them, evaluating and improving them.

● Give children cut-up copies of the original text (with numbers removed). Ask them first to match the diagrams to the written instructions, and then to sequence them.

Extension/further reading

Use contexts from other curriculum areas to write instructions in design and technology, for example. Give and write out instructions for making other types of books for presentation of writing across the curriculum. Ask children to write instructions in classroom contexts, such as how to use particular programs on the computer. Paul Johnson's *A Book of One's Own* (Hodder & Stoughton) has instructions for making many different books.

2: 1: T11: to use language of time (see sentence level work) to structure a sequence of events, e.g. *'when I had finished...'*, *'suddenly...'*, *'after that...*

2:1: T15: to write simple instructions, e.g. getting to school, playing a game

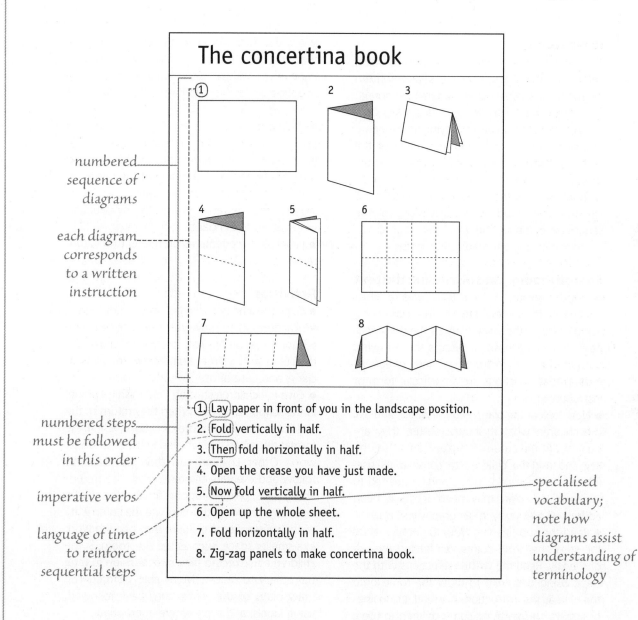

The concertina book

numbered sequence of diagrams

each diagram corresponds to a written instruction

numbered steps must be followed in this order

imperative verbs

language of time to reinforce sequential steps

1. Lay paper in front of you in the landscape position.
2. Fold vertically in half.
3. Then fold horizontally in half.
4. Open the crease you have just made.
5. Now fold vertically in half.
6. Open up the whole sheet.
7. Fold horizontally in half.
8. Zig-zag panels to make concertina book.

specialised vocabulary; note how diagrams assist understanding of terminology

2:1: T16: to use models from reading to organise instructions sequentially, e.g. listing points in order, each point depending on the previous one, numbering

2: 1: T17: to use diagrams in instructions, e.g. drawing and labelling diagrams as part of a set of instructions

2: 1: S2: to find examples, in fiction and non-fiction, of words and phrases that link sentences, e.g. *after, meanwhile, during, before, then, next, after a while*

Following directions

Background

This text presents opportunities to develop children's ability to read plans and written instructions. The plan offers a familiar context; it is simple and clear and includes a key as a means of organising and clarifying information. The written instructions include many of the features common to instructional texts – title, statement of purpose and sequenced steps in chronological order, imperative verbs, and linking words and phrases reinforcing the sequence in time. The text has clear cross-curricular links to geography and maths.

Shared reading and discussing the text

● Before looking at the text, give a child directions to somewhere in the classroom, using some of the vocabulary of the text (*first, next, turn right, past...*). Discuss this, drawing out the words *instructions* and *directions* (noting that directions are a particular form of instructions).

● Now look at the plan, read the labels, and ask the children what it shows (ensure they are clear about the nature of a plan). Focus on the key and ask the children to consider its use. (The knowledge and understanding needed to interpret the plan may need to have been addressed previously in geography lessons.)

● Read the sub-heading *How to get to...* Note the start and finish points, reinforcing the use of the key. Read the written directions with the class, using one child to draw the route onto the plan as the instructions are read, using lines or arrows. (It may assist some children to use a large version of the plan on the floor, so that they can physically follow the directions.)

● Cut up the written instructions and ask the children to reorder them without the use of the plan, which will prove difficult! Find the clues that will give some assistance – *First, Finally, library* (which links lines 2 and 3). Note that the directions have to be used in conjunction with the plan. Ask the children to consider what would make it easier to sequence the directions – numbering, for example.

● Ask the children to find the words in the text that tell you what to do. Highlight the imperatives. Now draw attention to the direction words that work with the imperatives – *out, right, along...*

● Highlight, in a different colour, words and phrases that indicate the sequence of the instructions (*First, Then, At the library...*), noting their position at the beginning of the sentence. Note the comma that separates the 'time' words and phrases from the instruction (imperative) to aid clarity.

● Label all these features on the text for future reference.

Activities

● Give the children sets of instructions (in a similar format) to move from one place in the school to another. Ask them to follow the directions and then evaluate them in terms of clarity and ease of use.

● Give the children starting and finishing points in the school to follow. When they return to the classroom, they can write directions, using the format described and labelled in the shared text work. Other children can then be asked to follow and evaluate the directions. Use mixed-ability pairs, provide support for the less able to work as a group, or differentiate the complexity of the routes. Some children may need to work in a smaller space, such as the classroom. Some children could record their directions on to tape for others to follow. More able children can draw plans of the routes they have followed, using labels, and a key where appropriate.

● Using a simple plan of your school, ask the children to mark routes on it and write directions for the routes.

Extension/further reading

Provide the children with maps and plans from work in geography to mark routes and write directions. See, for example, *Scholastic Teacher Bookshop: Making and Using Maps*. Use mazes (on paper or marked on the playground) to give and write directions.

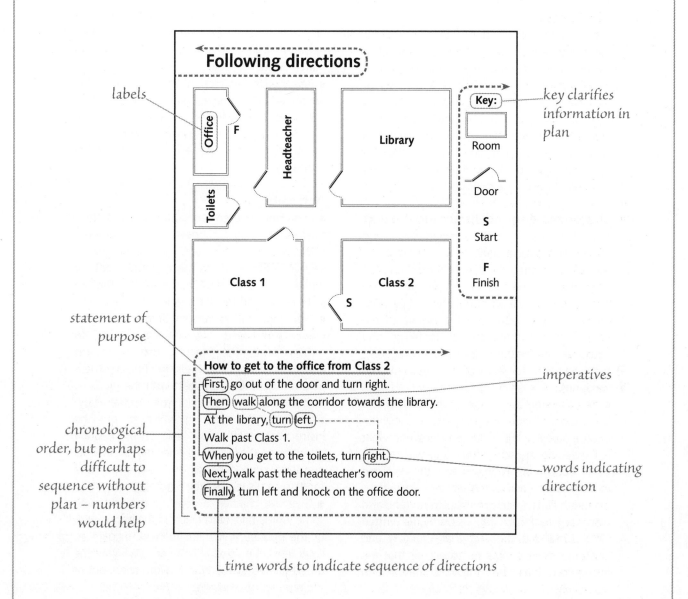

Following directions

labels

Office **F**

Toilets

Headteacher

Library

Class 1

Class 2

S

Key:

Room

Door

S Start

F Finish

key clarifies information in plan

statement of purpose

chronological order, but perhaps difficult to sequence without plan – numbers would help

How to get to the office from Class 2

First, go out of the door and turn right.
Then walk along the corridor towards the library.
At the library, turn left.
Walk past Class 1.
When you get to the toilets, turn right.
Next, walk past the headteacher's room
Finally, turn left and knock on the office door.

imperatives

words indicating direction

time words to indicate sequence of directions

Felt finger puppets

Background

This instructional text, giving the procedure for making a fabric finger puppet, will appeal to children, and the language is simple and direct, while introducing topic-related vocabulary. It has clear links to puppet-making units in design and technology, and to properties of materials in science, allowing literacy to be related to other curriculum work. The text incorporates many of the organisational and linguistic features typical of the genre.

Shared reading and discussing the text

● Read the text with the children, explaining any unfamiliar vocabulary.

● Ask the children to identify the sections of the text, using sub-headings to navigate. Label the title (which is also the statement of purpose – what is to be achieved), the picture of the finished puppet, the list of materials and equipment needed, the numbered instructions, the illustrations for some of the steps, and the variations.

● Cover the text and consider whether it would be possible to make the puppet using only the illustrations. Ask the children to describe what is happening in each picture and write down their suggestions. Now uncover the text and identify places where the written instructions extend the information in the pictures (and also places where the illustrations clarify the written text). Draw out the fact that the text and illustrations work together to ensure that the instructions can be followed easily and accurately.

● Add labels to the first two illustrations to show how this can further clarify the process, demonstrating how to use lines to point to parts of the picture and adding a brief explanation of each.

● Focus on the list of materials, highlighting the bullet points. Note that bullets are a way of distinguishing items in a list. Rewrite the items along a single line, using commas to separate (noting that the commas replace the bullets). Ask the children to consider which is more

effective. Draw out the point that a vertical list allows items to be considered one at a time and perhaps ticked off to ensure that all the materials are available.

● Read each instruction and highlight the action required – the imperatives – noting their position at the beginning of the sentence. Note that some of the steps have more than one sentence, where further explanation is needed for clarity.

Activities

● In groups, children can follow the instructions to make the finger puppets, then evaluate the effectiveness of the text, considering each section. Ask them to suggest improvements or additions to the list of materials, the written instructions and the illustrations.

● Prepare a cut-up version of the text (with numbers removed) and ask the children to reassemble it, first matching text to pictures and then sequencing the instructions. For less able children, leave the text with the pictures. In guided work, ask children to explain how they knew the order in which to put the instructions. With more able children, draw attention to the language clues that show how one instruction depends on the previous one for its sense (such as *Draw another line*).

● Give the children a copy of the text with some words taken out (such as the imperatives or the nouns). Ask them to work in pairs to complete the text. This activity can be differentiated by the type of word taken out or the number of omissions.

● Ask children to add labels to each illustration, using the model begun in the shared text work.

Extension/further reading

Children can write their own instructions for similar activities, incorporating the identified features. See *Making Puppets* by Josie McKinnon (Rigby Educational) and *365 Rainy Day Activities* by Vivienne Bolton (Dempsey Parr) for other puppet-making ideas.

2: 1: T13: to read simple written instructions in the classroom, simple recipes, plans, instructions for constructing something

2: 1: T14: to note key structural features, e.g. clear statement of purpose at start, sequential steps set out in a list, direct language

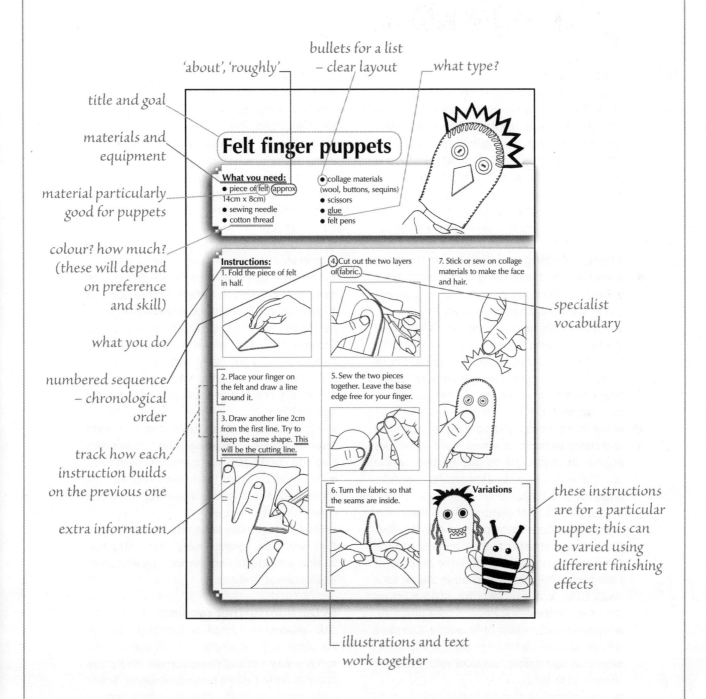

bullets for a list – clear layout

'about', 'roughly'

what type?

title and goal

materials and equipment

material particularly good for puppets

colour? how much? (these will depend on preference and skill)

what you do

numbered sequence – chronological order

track how each instruction builds on the previous one

extra information

specialist vocabulary

these instructions are for a particular puppet; this can be varied using different finishing effects

illustrations and text work together

Felt finger puppets

What you need:
- piece of felt (approx 14cm x 8cm)
- sewing needle
- cotton thread
- collage materials (wool, buttons, sequins)
- scissors
- glue
- felt pens

Instructions:

1. Fold the piece of felt in half.

2. Place your finger on the felt and draw a line around it.

3. Draw another line 2cm from the first line. Try to keep the same shape. <u>This will be the cutting line.</u>

4. Cut out the two layers of fabric.

5. Sew the two pieces together. Leave the base edge free for your finger.

6. Turn the fabric so that the seams are inside.

7. Stick or sew on collage materials to make the face and hair.

Variations

2: 1: T16: to use models from reading to organise instructions sequentially, e.g. listing points in order, each point depending on the previous one, numbering

2: 1: T17: to use diagrams in instructions, e.g. drawing and labelling diagrams as part of a set of instructions

How to play Boxes

Background

'Boxes' is a game played by many children. Since it requires few resources, it can be played almost anywhere. Most children will have learned to play the game through oral instructions and observation of others. This text presents written instructions for the game. The text provides a simple introduction to instructions for playing games, which can be extended to games that are more complex.

Shared reading and discussing the text

● Read the text with the children. Allow them to discuss among themselves their experiences of this game, and how they learned to play it.

● Select a child who has not played the game before and ask him or her to follow the instructions and play the game on the board. (If none of the children is familiar with the game, they could each have a set of instructions and play in pairs.)

● Ask the children to evaluate the effectiveness and clarity of the instructions. If the game was played successfully, share the features of the text that ensured success. If it was not, consider what the difficulties were.

● Identify and label features of the text – the title, introductory sentence, resources needed, the written instructions, the diagrams and the concluding sentence. Consider the purpose of each part of the text. Ask whether the sections could come in any other order. Make a list on the board of these features and their purpose.

● Note the bulleted list of resources. Compare this layout with a list written along a single line, separated by commas. Consider which is easier to read and use.

● Discuss how the diagrams help. Look carefully at the written text and suggest parts that might not be clear without the diagram. Consider whether the diagrams alone would enable someone to play the game.

● Highlight the imperatives, which state the action to be taken, noting that numbers 3 and 4 are not direct instructions but sum up the aim of the game.

Activities

● Choose a game that the children know (perhaps a playground game or 'Noughts and Crosses'). Use shared writing to compose instructions for the game, drawing on the list of features identified earlier and using modelling, scribing and supported composition. Consider the need to add supplementary information and whether diagrams would improve the instructions.

● The children should now be able to write their own instructions independently (in pairs) for another game of their choice. Encourage more able children to write for more complex games, where instructions and diagrams may need to be more detailed and precise. Less able children may need to play the game selected and, with support, write instructions during each stage of the game. Writing frames and identifying key features will also support less able children.

● Ask children to swap texts and play each other's games, following the instructions carefully. Let the players suggest improvements.

● Use guided writing to re-read and edit for sense and punctuation, modelling with one child's (or pair's) text.

● Children can make large reference charts for the classroom, giving 'rules' for instruction writing and identifying the key organisational and language features.

Extension/further reading

Ask children to write instructions for the classroom – for example, how to start up the computer or get out PE equipment. In PE, use imperatives to explore movement words. Books with instructions for playing games include *Casting the Dice* by Fran Mosley (BEAM Education), *Children's Games in Street and Playground* by Iona and Peter Opie (OUP) and *The Children's Party Book* by Anne and Peter Thomas (Floris Books). Children can follow and evaluate instructions for some of these games, considering the range of ways in which they are presented.

2: 1: T13: to read simple written instructions in the classroom, simple recipes, plans, instructions for constructing something

2: 1: T14: to note key structural features, e.g. clear statement of purpose at start, sequential steps set out in a list, direct language

title and statement of purpose

introduction appealing and enticing reader

sub-heading

bulleted list

imperatives

numbered sequence – chronological order

specialist vocabulary, note that diagram demonstrates terminology

supplementary advice

supplementary information, again addressing reader directly

diagram to aid understanding

not direct instructions so no imperative: summing up aim of game

addressing reader

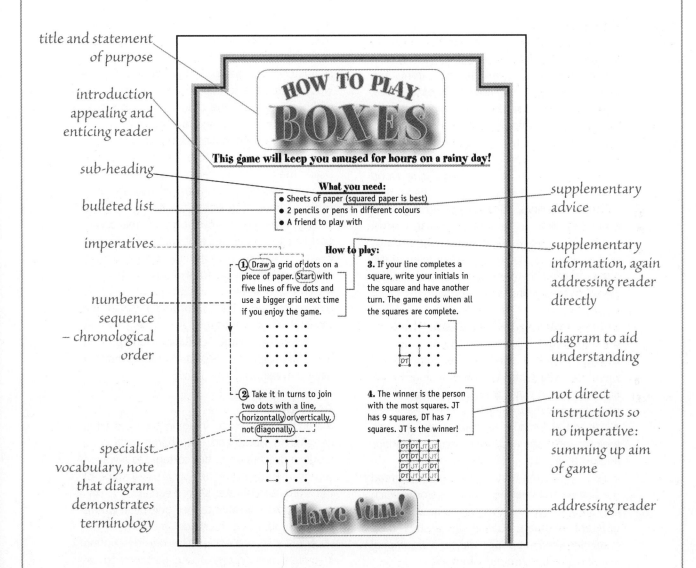

2: 1: T15: to write simple instructions, e.g. getting to school, playing a game

2: 1: T17: to use diagrams in instructions, e.g. drawing and labelling diagrams as part of a set of instructions

2: 1: S4: to re-read own writing for sense and punctuation

Little Red Riding Hood

retold by Helen Oxenbury

Extract 1

126

Background

Traditional tales are an important genre of children's literature, many originating in an oral storytelling culture. The children's parents and grandparents will also know many of the tales, which gives a sense of shared experience. As the tales were passed on and written down, changes occurred, giving rise to many different versions. This extract from Helen Oxenbury's simply told version of *Little Red Riding Hood* allows the children to compare the openings of different retellings. Characters, settings and events are likely to be broadly similar, even if some of the details are different. The settings of the tale are crucial to the development of the plot, and offer the opportunity to develop this aspect of the children's own writing.

Shared reading and discussing the text

● Before beginning work on the text, get the children to ask a parent/grandparent to tell them the story of Little Red Riding Hood, noting where it varies from other versions they have heard or read.

● Ask the children to tell each other in pairs, their version of the story, then discuss similarities and differences.

● Tell the children that they are going to read the first part of one version of the story, which may be the same as theirs in some ways and different in others. Why might a story have many versions? Introduce the term *traditional tale* and give background information.

● Read the extract with the children, stopping at some words to discuss the strategies used to read them, drawing out use of grammar and context as well as graphophonic cues. Consider specifically the way in which compound words can be split to help with reading and understanding. Highlight *woodcutter*, look for its two parts, and consider the meanings of each part and of the complete word.

● Ask the children to predict what will happen next in this version of Little Red Riding Hood, using the clues in the text.

● Discuss similarities and differences between this and other versions. It is likely that the similarities will include key features, such as the characters (with the possible exception of the woodcutter), the setting, and the events so far (although some of the children's versions may not have the wolf eating grandmother).

● Ask the children to discuss in pairs where the story happens and to note the three settings. Divide the class into three groups and ask each to write words or phrases to describe one setting, considering sights, sounds, smells and feelings. Share and write some on the board. Consider the significance of each setting. How would the story change if the wood was a town or the cottage a castle for example?

● Can the children tell what time of day it is? (The wolf says *'Good morning'.*) Could the story be set at night-time? Are there any clues to the weather? (Little Red Riding Hood puts on her cloak – perhaps it is cold. Would her mother have sent her out in the rain?)

Activities

● Ask the children to imagine they are Little Red Riding Hood and use shared writing to model a description of her cottage, as a way of setting the scene for the story, using some of the words and phrases shared earlier.

● Children can now write their own descriptions of the wood, using the model and some of the vocabulary shared earlier. Use one description in guided work (or response partners) to re-read for sense and accuracy. Less able writers could draw the setting and write words and phrases underneath or around the picture. Alternatively, they could use sentence starters, for example *I can see... I can hear...* Encourage more able writers to be adventurous with their vocabulary, for example by bringing in interesting adjectives.

● Ask mixed-ability pairs to find other compound words in the text, identifying the two words within them, and the meanings of the parts and the whole.

2: 2: T2: to use phonological, contextual, grammatical and graphic knowledge to work out, predict and check the meanings of unfamiliar words and to make sense of what they read

2: 2: T4: to predict story endings/incidents, e.g. from unfinished extracts, while reading with the teacher

2: 2: T5: to discuss story settings: to compare differences; to locate key words and phrases in text; to consider how different settings influence events and behaviour

Little Red Riding Hood *Extract 1*

traditional story opening

There was once a little girl whose mother made her a new cloak with a hood. It was a lovely red colour and she liked to wear it so much that everyone called her Little Red Riding Hood.

significant setting; dark woods often features in traditional stories

One day her mother said to her, "I want you to take this basket of cakes to your grandmother who is ill."

has given this warning before

clue to what will happen

Little Red Riding Hood liked to walk through the woods to her grandmother's cottage and she quickly put on her cloak. As she was leaving, her mother said, "Now remember, don't talk to any strangers on the way."

an obvious stranger, but Little Red Riding Hood still talks to him

time of day

But Little Red Riding Hood loved talking to people, and as she was walking along the path, she met a wolf.

wolf is flattering her

"Good morning, Little Girl, where are you off to in your beautiful red cloak?" said the wolf with a wicked smile.

preconceptions of wolves; clear he is going to be a 'bad' character

Little Red Riding Hood is not following her mother's instructions

Little Red Riding Hood put down her basket and said, "I'm taking some cakes to my grandmother who's not very well."

"Where does your grandmother live?" asked the wolf.

"In the cottage at the end of this path," said Little Red Riding Hood.

clue to character and intentions

small, cosy, comfortable

Now the wolf was really very hungry and he wanted to eat Little Red Riding Hood then and there. But he heard a woodcutter not far away and he ran off.

quite unaware of the danger

introduces the character who turns out to be the hero

He went straight to the grandmother's cottage where he found the old woman sitting up in bed. Before she knew what was happening, he ate her up in one gulp. Then he put on the grandmother's nightdress and her nightcap, and climbed into her bed. He snuggled well down under the bedclothes and tried to hide himself.

he is afraid of being caught

important because she is still alive – clue to ending

compound words

2: 2: T13: to use story settings from reading, e.g. re-describe, use in own writing, write a different story in the same setting

2: 2: S3: to re-read own writing to check for grammatical sense (coherence) and accuracy (agreement) – identify errors and suggest alternative constructions

2: 2: W4: to split familiar oral and written compound words into their component parts, e.g. *himself, handbag, milkman, pancake, teaspoon*

Little Red Riding Hood

retold by Helen Oxenbury

Background

Modern retellings often seek to sanitise some of the more gruesome details characteristic of traditional tales. The conclusion of this version retains elements of horror, but with the traditional happy ending. The text employs the familiar refrain in the dialogue between the wolf and the girl, which all the children will be able to repeat and enjoy. The clues in the first extract can be followed through, as the woodcutter comes to the rescue, and Little Red Riding Hood and her grandmother are found alive inside the wolf. The children can again compare versions, since it is the ending which is most often different, and consider characters, noting the clear divide between good and evil, and the consequences for each – a key theme of traditional stories.

Shared reading and discussing the text

● Remind the children of the first extract (re-reading if necessary) and ask them to review their predictions and the clues they used.

● Read this extract with the children, encouraging all to join in with the dialogue.

● Discuss the ending, and the similarities and differences between this version and others the children know. Consider why some might not include the more gruesome parts. Ask for views on which they prefer and why.

● Ask for views on the behaviour of Little Red Riding Hood and then focus on the ending again, considering how the events of the story might affect the subsequent behaviour of Red Riding Hood.

● Consider the justice of the wolf's end. Ask the children to consider other traditional tales where evil characters receive just treatment.

● Highlight words that contain the vowel phoneme *or*. Ask the children to identify the common sound. List words from the text in four columns, one for each spelling. Brainstorm other words containing the *or* phoneme and ask the children to write them on whiteboards, choosing the correct spelling. Note other spellings that arise (such as *caught, for*).

Activities

● Ask the children in pairs to brainstorm words and phrases that describe the wolf, his behaviour and character. Share some and write them on the board. Now look again at the text and ask the children to identify the evidence to support their descriptions. Refer to the first extract to develop this. Use some of these ideas to model sentences that describe the wolf's appearance and character, to be used below for posters.

● Children can make 'Stranger Danger' posters, to help others recognise and avoid the wolf, making clear why he is a danger. They should draw on words and phrases shared earlier, and build on the modelled sentences. Encourage more able children to use evidence from the text to provide detailed descriptions of the wolf, his character and behaviour. Give less able children a frame for writing, using headings or sentence starters.

● Use guided reading to re-read the story, focusing on the strategies used to make sense of the text. More able readers could read and compare other versions of the story and express preferences.

● Give the children cut-up versions of both extracts to reassemble. The children should work in groups to encourage discussion on how they know the order of the sections. The children could work in mixed-ability groups for sequencing, or the activity could be differentiated by the length of text provided (how it is cut up).

Extension/further reading

Children can role-play the story in groups of six (characters and narrator), drawing on the language of the original. Make posters or prompt cards to remind others about strategies to read unfamiliar words. Read other traditional tales with similar settings, themes or characters for comparison. See, for example, *The Helen Oxenbury Nursery Story Book* (Egmont) and *The Fairy Tale Treasury*, selected by Virginia Haviland, Hamish (Random House).

2: 2: T3: to discuss and compare story themes

2: 2: T6: to identify and describe characters, expressing own views and using words and phrases from texts

2: 2: T14: to write character profiles, e.g. simple descriptions, posters, passports, using key words and phrases that describe or are spoken by characters in the text

connects to previous extract

Little Red Riding Hood's name for her grandmother (like Mum for mother)

note use of repeated 'What big...' to build up suspense

should she have run away at this point?

pretence is over

lucky chance

wouldn't they have been very frightened, if not injured?

what might her mother say?

Little Red Riding Hood *Extract 2*

Before long, Little Red Riding Hood came to the door with her basket of cakes and knocked.

"Come in," said the wolf, trying to make his voice sound soft.

At first, when she went in, Little Red Riding Hood thought that her grandmother must have a bad cold.

She went over to the bed. "What big eyes you have, Grandmama," she said, as the wolf peered at her from under the nightcap.

"All the better to see you with, my dear," said the wolf.

"What big ears you have, Grandmama."

"All the better to hear you with, my dear," said the wolf.

Then Little Red Riding Hood saw a long nose and a wide-open mouth. She wanted to scream but she said, very bravely, "What a big mouth you have, Grandmama."

At this the wolf opened his jaws wide. "All the better to eat you with!" he cried. And he jumped out of bed and ate up Little Red Riding Hood.

Just at that moment the woodcutter passed by the cottage. Noticing that the door was open, he went inside. When he saw the wolf he quickly swung his axe and chopped off his head.

Little Red Riding Hood and then her grandmother stepped out, none the worse for their adventure.

Little Red Riding Hood thanked the woodcutter and ran home to tell her mother all that had happened. And after that day, she never, ever, spoke to strangers.

'or' phoneme

wolf's voice usually deep, growly and gruff

term of affection – deceitful

big clue – gives the game away

cruel? gruesome? just?

polite

learned her lesson

repeated for emphasis

2: 2: W2: the common spelling patterns for the vowel phonemes: *'air'*, *'or'*, *'er'* (Appendix List 3):
● to identify the phonemes in speech and writing
● to blend the phonemes for reading
● to segment the words into phonemes for spelling

Brer Rabbit and the Tar Baby

retold by
Julius Lester

Extract 1

Background

Uncle Remus was the pen-name of American writer Joel Chandler Harris, who wrote down the stories he had heard in his childhood, in the Deep South of America, 150 years ago. The theme is often seen as analogous to slaves outwitting their masters (the apparently weak outmanoeuvring the strong by wit and cunning). The tales all centre upon Brer Fox's attempts to catch Brer Rabbit for the cooking pot, and Brer Rabbit's talent for trickery and escape. (Many children will be able to make links with similar themes in other stories, such as cartoon stories of Bugs Bunny and Wile E Coyote, and others.) The story of the Tar Baby is perhaps the most well-known of the stories, and tells of Brer Fox's plan to trap Brer Rabbit by getting him stuck to his 'baby' made of tar. Julius Lester's retelling retains many echoes of the original African-American English dialect in the narrative and dialogue, allowing the children to explore uses of English, and to enjoy the language when reading aloud.

Shared reading and discussing the text

● Give the children background information as appropriate, noting particularly that, like other traditional tales, this is a retelling (of a retelling!). Set the scene by talking about the theme of Brer Rabbit stories, and allowing discussion of the children's experiences of similar stories. Introduce this text by explaining Brer Fox's plan with the Tar Baby.

● Read the text aloud to the children, perhaps more than once (with appropriate accent if possible!).

● Ask the children to discuss and retell the story in pairs. Ask one child to retell to the class. Consider how their retellings differ from the original, drawing out the language used.

● Highlight some non-standard phrases and ask the children to consider how they might say or write them. Draw attention to their use as part of an American dialect that is often different to the English we speak and write.

● Phrases such as *ain't* and *teach you no manners* may be part of some children's spoken dialect. Note that we don't usually use such phrases in writing, but they are used here to give a feel for the voice of the storyteller and characters.

● Ask the children to discuss Brer Rabbit's character, drawing on the evidence in narrative and dialogue. Focus initially on the phrase *strutting along…* What does this tell us about Brer Rabbit? Ask the children to describe his character, noting the parts of the text that show this.

● Re-read the text together, stopping at particular points, and asking the children to point out features on the page that tell them how to read it aloud – commas, exclamation/ question marks, italic, capitals, *yelled*. While reading, model how to break longer words into syllables for decoding.

● Ask the children to predict what might happen next, drawing on their experience of other stories. Do they think Brer Fox will trap and eat Brer Rabbit? If not, how might he escape?

Activities

● Children can begin character profiles of Brer Rabbit, using suggestions made earlier and adding their own. Tell them that they will add to these when they have read more of the story (see extract 2, page 48). Less able children could use a picture of Brer Rabbit and write short words and phrases around it. More able children should be encouraged to use phrases from the text, considering the way Brer Rabbit might describe himself.

● Give the children copies of the text and ask them to find all the words and phrases not normally found in writing, and rewrite them. Use the plenary to read aloud some rewritten texts and compare them with the original, drawing out the different 'voice'. Give less able children copies of the text with non-standard language highlighted.

2: 2: S2: to read aloud with intonation and expression appropriate to the grammar and punctuation (sentences, speech marks, exclamation marks)

2: 2: S4: to be aware of the need for grammatical agreement in speech and writing, matching verbs to nouns/pronouns correctly, e.g. *I am; the children are*

2: 2: W5: to discriminate, orally, syllables in multi-syllabic words using children's names and words from their reading, e.g. *dinosaur, family, dinner, children.* Extend to written forms and note syllable boundary in speech and writing

short for brother (dialect) – common title in traditional tales from various cultures

a doll made out of tar ; sticky – whoever touches it will become stuck to it!

decode syllables for reading

to make it more realistic

common in some speech dialects; not normally written

big-headed, laughing at his own jokes

voice of narrator (storyteller) who of course wrote the joke!

looking forward to Brer Rabbit's capture

demonstrates how to read the dialogue; reflects Brer Rabbit's ignorance

walking in a proud way; reveals a lot about Rabbit's character – confident and pleased with himself

italic to show he is shouting

double negatives; non-standard dialect

takes a swing

change to present tense gives sense of action; unusual in writing – normally need consistent verb tense

sudden sound of fist hitting wet sticky tar

what happens next?

so angry he's not thinking straight; he can't see what the Tar Baby really is

BRER RABBIT AND THE TAR BABY

Extract 1

BRER FOX TOOK his Tar Baby down to the road, the very road Brer Rabbit walked along every morning. He sat the Tar Baby in the road, put a hat on it, and then hid in a ditch.

He had scarcely gotten comfortable (as comfortable as one can get in a ditch), before Brer Rabbit came strutting along like he owned the world and was collecting rent from everybody in it.

Seeing the Tar Baby, Brer Rabbit tipped his hat. "Good morning! Nice day, ain't it? Of course, any day I wake up and find I'm still alive is a nice day as far as I'm concerned." He laughed at his joke, which he thought was pretty good. (Ain't too bad if I say so myself.)

Tar Baby don't say a word. Brer Fox stuck his head up out of the ditch, grinning.

"You deaf?" Brer Rabbit asked the Tar Baby. "If you are, I can talk louder." He yelled, *"How you this morning? Nice day, ain't it?"*

Tar Baby still don't say nothing.

Brer Rabbit was getting kinna annoyed. "I don't know what's wrong with this young generation. Didn't your parents teach you no manners?"

Tar Baby don't say nothing.

"Well, I reckon I'll teach you some!" He hauls off and hits the Tar Baby. BIP! And his fist was stuck to the side of the Tar Baby's face.

"You let me go!" Brer Rabbit yelled. "Let me go or I'll really pop you one." He twisted and turned, but he couldn't get loose. "All right! I warned you!" And he smacked the Tar Baby on the other side of the head. BIP! His other fist was stuck.

2: 2: T3: to discuss and compare story themes

2: 2: T4: to predict story endings/incidents, e.g. from unfinished extracts, while reading with the teacher

2: 2: T6: to identify and describe characters, expressing own views and using words and phrases from texts

2: 2: T14: to write character profiles, e.g. simple descriptions, posters, passports, using key words and phrases that describe or are spoken by characters in the text

Brer Rabbit and the Tar Baby

retold by Julius Lester

Extract 2

Background

Here we see that Brer Fox's plan has worked – Brer Rabbit has continued to hit the Tar Baby and is now firmly stuck by all four paws and his head! Brer Rabbit pretends to be frightened, but clearly has a plan for escape, and he talks Brer Fox out of his intended methods for the kill. Brer Rabbit repeatedly begs not to be thrown in the 'briar patch', and Brer Fox is fooled into believing that this will be the worst fate possible. The children may be able to predict the inevitable outcome. The language of this second extract continues to reflect the voice of the storyteller and develops the characters of Brer Rabbit and Brer Fox.

Shared reading and discussing the text

● Remind the children of the first extract, asking them to retell it and recall their predictions, re-reading if necessary.

● Read the text with the children, drawing on features of expression and intonation noted in the first extract. Remind them of the use of syllabification to decode longer words. Ask the children to identify non-standard language, referring to work on the first extract.

● Ask the children to write (on whiteboards) the key stages of the plot, using arrows to indicate sequence. Highlight in the text each of Brer Fox's plans and the reason for abandoning it, and illustrate this in two columns.

● Discuss Brer Rabbit's response to each idea. Why does he repeatedly plead not to be thrown in the briar patch? If necessary, remind the children of similar stories, and draw out Brer Rabbit's trickery.

● Ask the children to discuss in pairs what might happen. How might he respond to the threat of being skinned? Is he thrown in the briar patch? Is this the end of him?

● Consider what we learn about Brer Rabbit, building on the work done on the first extract. Ask the children to brainstorm words and phrases, identifying evidence in the extract.

● Ask the children for their views on Brer Fox, suggesting words and phrases to describe him.

Activities

● In shared writing, use the chart made earlier to plan two more ideas for killing Brer Rabbit, and predict his responses. Model the next two or three sentences, using appropriate language. Point out dialect usage and demonstrate the standard equivalent. Make some deliberate mistakes in tense and subject/verb agreement, and ask the children to correct them. Discuss a conclusion and include it in the plan, considering Brer Rabbit's response to being thrown in the briar patch and his escape.

● Ask the children to write their own continuations of the story (in pairs or small groups), using the plan and model from shared writing. Less able children can copy the modelled sentences and add one more idea. Compose an ending in guided writing.

● Ask the children to continue their character profiles of Brer Rabbit started in extract 1, adding new information. They may wish to do a character profile of Brer Fox. Ask them to compare the two characters and consider whether they are 'good' or 'bad' (or perhaps both). Encourage them to state which one they prefer and why. For less able children, provide a frame for expressing views on characters, for example *I like Brer Rabbit best because…*

● Children can role-play the story, incorporating their endings, once written.

Extension/further reading

Use hot-seating to find out more about each character. Ask some children to take on the role of Brer Rabbit, telling the story from his point of view, to a set of newspaper reporters. Read other traditional stories with a similar theme, for example 'The Gingerbread Boy', 'The Three Little Pigs', 'The Three Billy Goats Gruff' (all available in *The Helen Oxenbury Nursery Story Book*, Egmont) and 'The Wolf and the Seven Little Kids' in *The Fairy Tale Treasury*, selected by Virginia Haviland (Random House). Collections of traditional stories from other cultures include *A Twist in the Tail* by Mary Hoffman (Frances Lincoln).

2: 2: S5: to use verb tenses with increasing accuracy in speaking and writing

2: 2: T4: to predict story endings/ incidents, e.g. from unfinished extracts, while reading with the teacher

part of his act to deceive Brer Fox

repeats the phrase often

pretending to be casual and accepting of his fate

not enough just to kill and eat him; he's frustrated by previous failed attempts

again pretending

still pretending

= I've got it

BRER RABBIT AND THE TAR BABY

Extract 2

"I guess I'm going to be barbecued this day." Brer Rabbit sighed. "But getting barbecued is a whole lot better than getting thrown in the briar patch." He sighed again. "No doubt about it. Getting barbecued is almost a blessing compared to being thrown into that briar patch on the other side of the road. If you got to go, go in a barbecue sauce. That's what I always say. How much lemon juice and brown sugar you put in yours?"

When Brer Fox heard this, he had to do some more thinking, because he wanted the worst death possible for that rabbit. "Now that I thinks on it, it's too hot to be standing over a hot fire. I think I'll hang you."

Brer Rabbit shuddered. "Hanging is a terrible way to die! Just terrible! But I thank you for being so considerate. Hanging is better than being thrown in the briar patch."

Brer Fox thought that over a minute. "Come to think of it, I can't hang you, 'cause I didn't bring my rope. I'll drown you in the creek over yonder."

Brer Rabbit sniffed like he was about to cry. "No, no, Brer Fox. You know I can't stand water, but I guess drowning, awful as it is, is better than the briar patch."

"I got it!" Brer Fox exclaimed. "I don't feel like dragging you all the way down to the creek. I got my knife right here. I'm going to skin you!" He pulled out his knife.

a prickly bush; beginning of his trickery: rabbits are used to living in bushes and undergrowth

non-standard English

should Brer Fox realise he is being tricked?

stream

2: 2: T7: to prepare and retell stories individually and through role-play in groups, using dialogue and narrative from text

2: 2: T14: to write character profiles, e.g. simple descriptions, posters, passports, using key words and phrases that describe or are spoken by characters in the text

Rabbit and Tiger retold by Grace Hallworth

Background

Grace Hallworth grew up in Trinidad, and 'Rabbit and Tiger' is from her collection of traditional West Indian tales. The story is one of a series originating among the native tribes of South America, demonstrating the cross-cultural nature of traditional tales. They tell of the trickster, Konehu the rabbit, and his games with the other animals of the forest. In this story, Konehu has earlier played a trick on Tiger, who vows not to be caught out again, and determines to kill the rabbit. Konehu has another trick up his sleeve, however. At the end of the story, Tiger dives so deep that she does not resurface, and her fate is left in doubt. Comparisons can be made with other tales of trickery and cunning, familiar in many cultures, such as those of Brer Rabbit and Anancy.

Shared reading and discussing the text

● Set the context for the story using the information above. Discuss other stories with similar themes, where one creature (or human) outwits another.

● Read the text with the children, then re-read with two children taking the parts of the characters. Encourage the use of expression, using punctuation and text features. Remind them about the use of speech marks to indicate the words spoken by each character.

● Can the children explain Konehu's trick in their own words? (Remind them about reflections if necessary.) Ask them to close their eyes and imagine the sun reflected in the pool, to understand how the trick worked. Why was Tiger so anxious to fetch the golden ball from the pool? Note that Tiger thinks she is tricking Konehu!

● Ask the children to decide how the story ends. You might choose to tell them how Grace Hallworth's retelling concludes.

● Ask the children to work in pairs to identify features of the story setting, and use words and phrases, including those from the text, to describe them – the forest, the rock, the pool, and the reflection. Model how to turn some of the phrases into sentences, occasionally making then correcting mistakes, such as in verb tense.

Activities

● Brainstorm ideas for another story about Konehu. Choose another animal that might live in the forest. Consider what the trick might be and where in the forest it happens. (For example, Monkey might be tricked into climbing the highest tree to reach the sun in the sky.) Use shared writing to plan the new story, identifying characters, setting, the trick and the outcome.

● The children can now make plans for their own stories, drawing on ideas shared above. Less able children may need support to plan a group story. More able children should be encouraged to consider the setting carefully and its significance in their story.

● Put the children into mixed-ability pairs to plan a retelling of the story, first highlighting key phrases that they will incorporate.

● Use an art and design lesson to paint pictures of the forest, using evidence from the text. Then ask the children to turn words and phrases shared earlier into simple sentences about the setting. More able children should be imaginative with their descriptions and perhaps move beyond simple sentences to incorporate connectives.

● Use one plan to write a class story, or some children might write individual stories from their plans.

Extension/further reading

Read and compare other traditional stories with a theme of how natural phenomena occurred. Dramatise the story, using masks, and have the children's paintings as a backdrop. Read other traditional West Indian stories from Grace Hallworth's *Cric Crac* (Mammoth) and stories from other cultures, for example *A Twist in the Tail: Animal Stories from Around the World* by Mary Hoffman (Frances Lincoln), *My First Big Story Book* by Richard Bamberger (Puffin) and Rudyard Kipling's *Just So Stories* (Penguin).

2: 2: S3: to re-read own writing to check for grammatical sense (coherence) and accuracy (agreement) – identify errors and suggest alternative constructions

2: 2: S9: to secure the use of simple sentences in own writing

name from another culture

description of setting

note repetition for emphasis and to aid description

RABBIT AND TIGER

Now Tiger was determined to kill Konehu the rabbit, so day after day she roamed the forest looking for him.

One day she spotted the rabbit high, high up on a rock gazing into the forest pool below. The yellow sun overhead, reflected in the water, looked like a golden ball.

"Konehu, Konehu, I am coming to kill you!" roared Tiger.

"Oh Tiger, you are just in time to witness a wonderful sight," said Konehu.

Tiger climbed right up to the rock where Konehu sat.

"What are you looking at?" asked Tiger.

"See that golden ball in the pool?" said Konehu. "If only we could get it out we would be richer than the King."

Tiger looked down at the golden ball. It was so bright that it lit up the water in the pool.

"Konehu," she said, "you are too small to lift such a large ball. Let me go in and bring it up for you."

Tiger intended to run off with the gold and keep it all for herself.

"Very well," said Konehu, "but when you get it, hold it fast. Don't let it slip from you or it will go deeper."

Quickly Tiger dived into the pool, but she came up spluttering and snorting. She had not found the gold.

Konehu called to her:

"Tiger my friend, be brave, be bold.
Go deep and deep to find the gold."

So once more Tiger dived down, down into the pool, into the cool water, and once more Tiger rose puffing and blowing so hard that she sprayed Konehu where he sat high up on the rock.

Tiger was ready to give up the search, but Konehu shouted:

"Tiger, you must be brave and bold.
Go deeper still to find the gold."

reader perhaps knows that this will be another trick; the rabbit is not frightened of Tiger

Konehu knows how to play on Tiger's stupidity and greed

not-so-clever Tiger really believes it is a golden ball

Tiger thinks she is tricking Konehu

repetition to emphasise depth of water

simile

exclamation mark and 'roared' indicate how speech is uttered

curious Tiger is immediately fooled

chant to encourage Tiger

adjective for description

chant almost identical

2: 2: T5: to discuss story settings: to compare differences; to locate key words and phrases in text; to consider how different settings influence events and behaviour

2: 2: T7: to prepare and re-tell stories individually and through role-play in groups, using dialogue and narrative from text

2: 2: T13: to use story settings from reading, e.g. re-describe, use in own writing, write a different story in the same setting

The Little Red Hen and the Grain of Wheat

retold by Sara Cone Bryant

Background

This is a traditional tale with a very simple structure and plot, and a straightforward moral. The language is distinctive, with repeated refrains in dialogue and narrative, allowing children to predict and enjoy the patterns when reading aloud and through role-play. The phrase *'Not I'* is particularly characteristic of story language as distinct from everyday speech.

The story offers links to science and design and technology. In order to fully appreciate the text, children will need to learn about the bread-making process, from planting the seeds, harvesting, threshing and milling, through to making the bread itself, which might be done in an extension.

Shared reading and discussing the text

● Cover the last section of text (from *'Oh! I will…'*). Read the story aloud with the children, enjoying the patterns, and modelling appropriate expression, including voices for the characters. Pause and ask whether the hen will share the bread. Encourage the children to predict the actual words of the text. Finish the reading. Is this fair? Consider the 'moral'.

● Ask the children to express views on the repetitious structure and language. Highlight particularly *'Not I'* and consider how we might normally say it in speech.

● Give out cards, each with a sentence of dialogue on. Re-read the text, taking the part of narrator yourself, and ask the children with the relevant cards to stand up at the appropriate moments and read their cards aloud in character.

● Read the first sentence of the text again, then ask the child with the card to read what the hen said. Highlight this sentence. Ask the children what the marks at each end are for. Use a different colour to highlight the speech marks, and explain their use and purpose. Ask another child to find and read the next words spoken and to highlight these and the speech marks. Draw attention to *she said*, noting that this shows *who* is speaking. Repeat for the next three lines of dialogue.

● Put pictures of the four characters on the board. Demonstrate how to put the hen's words into a speech bubble, noting that this is another way of showing who is saying what. (Children may have experience of speech bubbles from comics for example.) Repeat for the words of the Duck, Cat and Dog.

Activities

● Children can draw a cartoon strip of the story, adding speech bubbles as above. Less able children can be given a prepared comic strip, with speech bubbles, in which to insert the words. More able children can caption the picture frames with the narrative.

● Ask the children to prepare a role-play of the story in groups, drawing on the language of the text, and the expression and intonation developed in guided reading.

● Ask mixed-ability pairs to match cards containing dialogue (in speech marks) to cards that state who said it. Use familiar dialogue from traditional tales. Add an element of nonsense by matching randomly (*'I'll huff and I'll puff…' said Goldilocks*).

Extension/further reading

Turn the role-plays into performances, by adding narrators, props and masks. Evaluate the performances, expressing views particularly on the effectiveness of the use of language and expression. The children can make posters for the classroom ('Two ways of showing who is saying what'), demonstrating the use of speech marks and speech bubbles. They can copy a short piece of text (perhaps from their own reading) onto the poster, put dialogue and speech marks in a different colour, and add an explanation; they can then draw a picture of the characters, put the dialogue into speech bubbles and again add an explanation.

The children can make bread, from recipes, making links to instruction texts from Term 1 (see page 32 onwards).

2: 2: S2: to read aloud with intonation and expression appropriate to the grammar and punctuation (sentences, speech marks, exclamation marks)

2: 2: S6: to identify speech marks in reading, understand their purpose, use the terms correctly

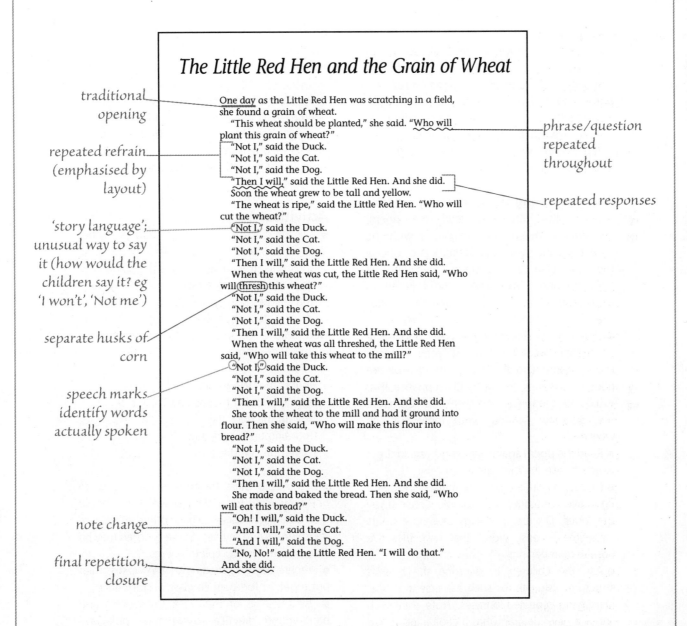

The Little Red Hen and the Grain of Wheat

traditional opening

One day as the Little Red Hen was scratching in a field, she found a grain of wheat.

"This wheat should be planted," she said. "Who will plant this grain of wheat?"

phrase/question repeated throughout

repeated refrain (emphasised by layout)

"Not I," said the Duck.
"Not I," said the Cat.
"Not I," said the Dog.
"Then I will," said the Little Red Hen. And she did.

repeated responses

Soon the wheat grew to be tall and yellow.
"The wheat is ripe," said the Little Red Hen. "Who will cut the wheat?"

'story language'; unusual way to say it (how would the children say it? eg 'I won't', 'Not me')

"Not I," said the Duck.
"Not I," said the Cat.
"Not I," said the Dog.
"Then I will," said the Little Red Hen. And she did.
When the wheat was cut, the Little Red Hen said, "Who will thresh this wheat?"
"Not I," said the Duck.
"Not I," said the Cat.
"Not I," said the Dog.
"Then I will," said the Little Red Hen. And she did.
When the wheat was all threshed, the Little Red Hen said, "Who will take this wheat to the mill?"

separate husks of corn

speech marks identify words actually spoken

"Not I," said the Duck.
"Not I," said the Cat.
"Not I," said the Dog.
"Then I will," said the Little Red Hen. And she did.
She took the wheat to the mill and had it ground into flour. Then she said, "Who will make this flour into bread?"
"Not I," said the Duck.
"Not I," said the Cat.
"Not I," said the Dog.
"Then I will," said the Little Red Hen. And she did.
She made and baked the bread. Then she said, "Who will eat this bread?"

note change

"Oh! I will," said the Duck.
"And I will," said the Cat.
"And I will," said the Dog.
"No, No!" said the Little Red Hen. "I will do that."

final repetition, closure

And she did.

2: 2: S7: to investigate and recognise a range of other ways of presenting texts, e.g. speech bubbles, enlarged, bold or italicised print, captions, headings and sub-headings

2: 2: T7: to prepare and retell stories individually and through role-play in groups, using dialogue and narrative from text

Come-day Go-day
by Barrie Wade

Background

This poem uses rhymes to describe each day of the week. The poet makes use of colloquial language and some less familiar words and phrases to add colour. This also provides the opportunity to introduce the children to figurative language. The verse structure is clear and patterned, with repeated lines, and there is a lively rhythm for reading aloud.

Shared reading and discussing the text

● Cover the title and read the poem, encouraging the children to join in with the repetitions and rhymes. (You might also conceal the last verse at this stage, predicting its structure and rhymes.) Ask the children to discuss possible titles, then share their ideas; then reveal the real title (and the last verse).

● Underline the days of the week and recite them together. What happens after Sunday? Draw attention to the cycle, noting how the poet uses *comes* and *goes* to emphasise this. Which are schooldays/the weekend? Compare the ideas for Monday with those for the weekend!

● Read the poem again, clapping a regular beat to emphasise the rhythms.

● Discuss any unfamiliar vocabulary, including figurative language, for example *Chase away the blues*. Discuss meanings and how poets sometimes choose words that have effective non-literal meanings.

● Ask the children to describe the poem's structure, using terms such as verse and line, identifying repeated phrases. Note that each line is a new idea, and has a capital letter and full stop.

● Ask the children to identify the rhymes in verse 1, as you read aloud again. Note that every line actually ends with *day*. Where does the rest of the rhyme occur? Emphasise the *sound* (listen, don't look at this point) at the end of the rhyming part. Draw attention to *m* rather than *n* in *glum,* telling the children that poets sometimes bend the rules and use a word that *nearly* rhymes, because the idea fits.

● Look closely at the spelling patterns of the rhymes, noting the *o* in *Monday,* rather than *u.*

● Repeat for other verses (identifying other half-rhymes). Use *Tuesday/Friday* to revise the long-vowel phonemes *oo/ie. Wednesday* may need a closer look; note its sound and irregular spelling. Use *Thursday* to introduce the *er* phoneme, brainstorming other words with this sound and investigating spellings. Note the extra syllable in *Saturday* and its rhymes.

Activities

● Ask the children, in pairs, to suggest rhymes (and half-rhymes) for each day, focusing on sounds first, then investigating the spelling of them. Model writing a new verse, using some of the children's suggestions. Ensure that there is plenty of talk about how to turn the rhyming word into a complete idea, maintaining the rhythm. For example:

> Here comes Wednesday.
> Playing with my friends day.
> Tidy up the pens day.
> Counting up in tens day.
> There goes Wednesday.

● In groups or pairs, the children can now write one new verse for a class poem. They should read aloud their verses to each other to evaluate the rhythms and rhymes. Some children may be able to compose complete poems.

● Prepare a group reading of the verses, then put together for a whole-class performance.

● Use the days of the week for spelling and handwriting practice, using the Look–Say–Cover–Write–Check method.

Extension/further reading

Set the poem to percussion instruments. Read other patterned poems to develop spelling of key words (days, months, numbers, colours). Suitable poems can be found in anthologies such as *Twinkle, Twinkle Chocolate Bar* (OUP), *Down by the River* (Mammoth), *Read Me* (Macmillan) and *The Works* (Macmillan).

2: 2: W1: to secure the reading and spelling of words containing different spellings of the long vowel phonemes from Year 1

2: 2: W2: the common spelling patterns for the vowel phonemes: 'air', 'or', 'er' (Appendix List 3):
● to identify the phonemes in speech and writing;
● to blend the phonemes for reading;
● to segment the words into phonemes for spelling

2: 2: W9: to spell common irregular words from Appendix List 1

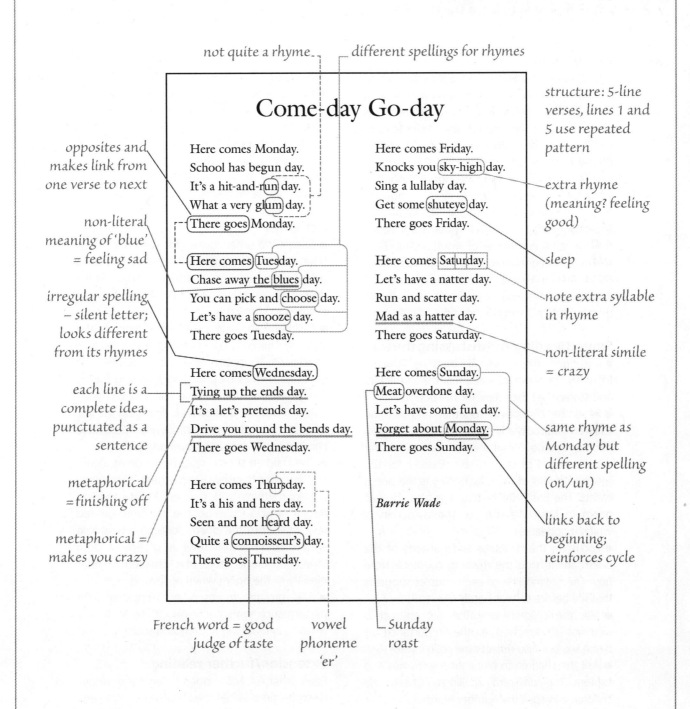

not quite a rhyme

different spellings for rhymes

Come-day Go-day

Here comes Monday.
School has begun day.
It's a hit-and-run day.
What a very glum day.
There goes Monday.

Here comes Tuesday.
Chase away the blues day.
You can pick and choose day.
Let's have a snooze day.
There goes Tuesday.

Here comes Wednesday.
Tying up the ends day.
It's a let's pretends day.
Drive you round the bends day.
There goes Wednesday.

Here comes Thursday.
It's a his and hers day.
Seen and not heard day.
Quite a connoisseur's day.
There goes Thursday.

Here comes Friday.
Knocks you sky-high day.
Sing a lullaby day.
Get some shuteye day.
There goes Friday.

Here comes Saturday.
Let's have a natter day.
Run and scatter day.
Mad as a hatter day.
There goes Saturday.

Here comes Sunday.
Meat overdone day.
Let's have some fun day.
Forget about Monday.
There goes Sunday.

Barrie Wade

opposites and makes link from one verse to next

non-literal meaning of 'blue' = feeling sad

irregular spelling – silent letter; looks different from its rhymes

each line is a complete idea, punctuated as a sentence

metaphorical = finishing off

metaphorical = makes you crazy

structure: 5-line verses, lines 1 and 5 use repeated pattern

extra rhyme (meaning? feeling good)

sleep

note extra syllable in rhyme

non-literal simile = crazy

same rhyme as Monday but different spelling (on/un)

links back to beginning; reinforces cycle

French word = good judge of taste

vowel phoneme 'er'

Sunday roast

2: 2: T8: to read own poems aloud

2: 2: T9: to identify and discuss patterns of rhythm, rhyme and other features of sound in different poems

2: 2: T15: to use structures from poems as a basis for writing, by extending or substituting elements, inventing own lines, verses; to make class collections, illustrate with captions; to write own poems from initial jottings and words

The End and Happiness

by AA Milne

Background

AA Milne is perhaps most famous as the creator of Winnie-the-Pooh and friends, but he also wrote many poems for young children. His poems reflect a comfortable middle-class childhood in the 1920s, some of which would appear to be quite alien to 21st-century children. However, the childhood thoughts, fantasies and feelings, told in simple language through the voice of Christopher Robin, are still accessible today. These two poems are about the joy and innocence of youth. 'The End' shares the delight of reaching the grand old age of six (which Year 2 children will recognise). 'Happiness' describes the simple pleasure of dressing for splashing in the rain.

Shared reading and discussing the text

● Introduce the poet. If possible, display Milne's work. Invite discussion of the characters and stories. Set the scene for the poems.
● Read the first poem together and ask the children to discuss and share their views. Is six a good age to be? What are the advantages and disadvantages of staying six? (Extend for the seven-year-olds in the class!) Why is the poem called 'The End'? (Note that it is also the last poem in *Now We Are Six*, the collection in which it appears.)
● Focus on the structure and patterns of the poem, identifying the rhyming couplets. Note how the second line of each couplet suggests that life before six was hardly life at all!
● Ask the children why the last couplet is different (it emphasises the importance of being six, but also reflects the child's voice).
● Ask the children to highlight the rhymes and explore the different spellings. Check the children can spell the number words.
● Read the second poem at least twice, with clear 'stamping' rhythm. Let the children stamp along! Share experiences of playing in the rain.
● Ask why the poem is called 'Happiness'. Focus on the effect of the last four lines, which round off the poem.

● Note the layout of the poem, the very short lines (each line has two beats to convey stamping) and initial capital letters, emphasising the importance (and size) of the clothes to John.
● Ask the children to discuss in pairs which of the two poems they prefer and why, encouraging them to refer to the rhythms, rhymes and language.

Activities

● Brainstorm other rhymes for each number in 'The End' and model writing a new poem, using some of the children's ideas. Make deliberate mistakes in verb tenses for the children to correct.
● Children can write their own poems, in the style of 'The End', using the last two lines as a conclusion. Support less able children to generate rhymes by providing a writing frame, using the structure of the original. Seven-year-olds will want to add a verse, changing the last couplet to read *now I am Seven*. More able children could continue beyond seven.
● The children should read their poems aloud, and evaluate their own and others, particularly noting rhythms and rhymes. Put poems on display and encourage the children to add reviews – *I like this poem because…* Less able writers could record reviews of poems onto tape; encourage more able children to refer directly to the poem when reviewing.
● Ask groups to prepare 'Happiness' for performance with particular attention to the rhythm, and adding actions and sounds.

Extension/further reading

Read other AA Milne poems; see, for example, the collections *When We Were Very Young* and *Now We Are Six* (Methuen) and *The Hums of Pooh* (Hamlyn Young Books). Children could copy favourites into a class book, with reasons for their choices. Use the Internet to research AA Milne, and prepare biographies to add to class anthologies.

2: 2: W6: to read on sight and spell all the words from Appendix List 1

2: 2: S5: to use verb tenses with increasing accuracy in speaking and writing, e.g. catch/caught, see/saw, go/went and to use past tense consistently for narration

2: 2: T9: to identify and discuss patterns of rhythm, rhyme and other features of sound in different poems

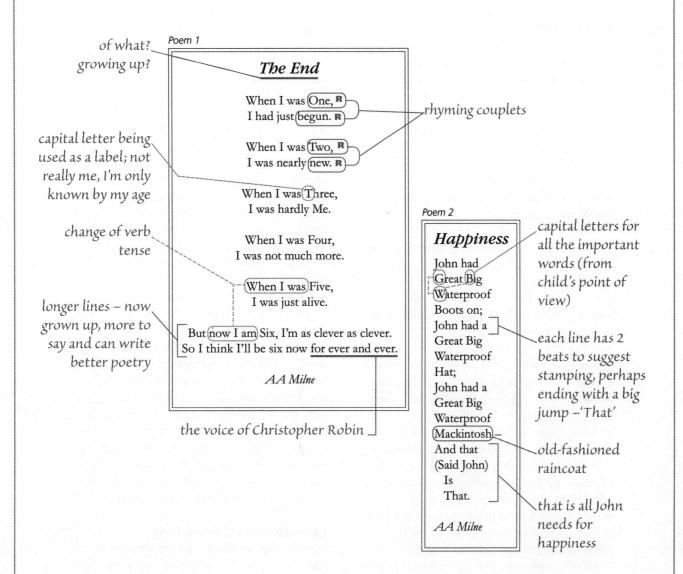

of what? growing up?

Poem 1

The End

When I was One, **R**
I had just begun. **R**

When I was Two, **R**
I was nearly new. **R**

When I was Three,
I was hardly Me.

When I was Four,
I was not much more.

When I was Five,
I was just alive.

But now I am Six, I'm as clever as clever.
So I think I'll be six now for ever and ever.

A A Milne

rhyming couplets

capital letter being used as a label; not really me, I'm only known by my age

change of verb tense

longer lines – now grown up, more to say and can write better poetry

the voice of Christopher Robin

Poem 2

Happiness

John had
Great Big
Waterproof
Boots on;
John had a
Great Big
Waterproof
Hat;
John had a
Great Big
Waterproof
Mackintosh –
And that
(Said John)
Is
That.

A A Milne

capital letters for all the important words (from child's point of view)

each line has 2 beats to suggest stamping, perhaps ending with a big jump – 'That'

old-fashioned raincoat

that is all John needs for happiness

2: 2: T11: to identify and discuss favourite poems and poets, using appropriate terms (poet, poem, verse, rhyme, etc.) and referring to the language of the poems

2: 2: T15: to use structures from poems as a basis for writing, by extending or substituting elements, inventing own lines, verses; to make class collections, illustrate with captions; to write own poems from initial jottings and words

Morning

by Grace Nichols

Background
Grace Nichols was born in Guyana but has lived in the UK for nearly 30 years. Much of her poetry reflects her roots, although here this voice is only noticeable right at the end. 'Morning' is a poem of sounds – the sounds of the morning. It has a rhythmic, onomatopoeic quality that will encourage the children to enjoy reading and reciting aloud. The structure is patterned and the context familiar, allowing the children to develop their own writing, based on the form and content.

Shared reading and discussing the text
● Read the poem aloud with the children, encouraging all to join in with the repeated phrases. Ask them to re-read in pairs (with support where needed), taking alternate lines. They could then swap parts and read again.
● Notice that in the penultimate verse, the speaker is *just listening* to the sounds. Ask them to close their eyes while you re-read the poem, and to imagine they are lying in bed listening to the same sounds.
● What is the effect of the last verse? Think of that moment when you can't lie and listen any longer; you have to get up! The longer line perhaps suggests that getting up has to disrupt the rhythm of the sounds.
● Ask the children to make notes on the form of the poem. Draw out features of the layout – the repeated phrases and the two-line verses. Why has the poet used no punctuation? Notice how it allows the poem to flow, perhaps suggesting the build up of the sounds, forcing you out of bed.
● Highlight phrases that describe the sounds. Prompt the children to hear the onomatopoeias (perhaps making them!). Ask them to count the syllables as you read each phrase, and then identify them within the words. Note the pattern of words and syllables in each line and the repeated -*ing* at the end. (They might note *popping/dropping, ringing/singing* as rhymes, where the other lines are not true rhymes.)

● Underline *milk-float, milkman, alarm-clock*. Note the way they can be split into two words (explain the hyphen), discussing how the whole word has the meaning of both parts in it.

Activities
● Share ideas from the children's own experience of the sounds of morning. Demonstrate how to turn some ideas into phrases in the same form as the poem, for example *sister showering*. Where single-syllable words have been suggested, model ways to retain the syllable pattern, for example *dog barking* might become *our dog barking*. Consider alternative phrases for the last line (*school-day morning*).
● Children can write their own poems, in pairs, beginning with a list of activities or sounds, and turning them into phrases, following the pattern of the poem. Less able children can work in a group with support, or in mixed-ability pairs, to compose and perform poems. Some might use a writing frame, where they add the two-word phrases. Encourage the children to read each line aloud to each other, as they compose, to evaluate the sense and rhythms, and, when the poems are complete, the children should prepare to perform them to the class, who will comment on their effect.

Extension/further reading
Begin a class anthology with poems by Grace Nichols, with comments and recommendations. Further poems from other cultures can be added as the children read them. Children can begin personal anthologies of poems they have particularly enjoyed, explaining why. Poems by Grace Nichols can be found in her collections *The Poet Cat* (Bloomsbury) and *Come into my Tropical Garden* (Young Lions). Her poems, as well as others from different cultures, can also be found in the anthologies *No Hickory, No Dock* (Puffin) and *A Caribbean Dozen*, both edited by John Agard and Grace Nichols (Walker Books).

2: 2: W4: to split familiar oral and written compound words into their component parts, e.g. *himself, handbag, milkman, pancake, teaspoon*

2: 2: W5: to discriminate, orally, syllables in multi-syllabic words using children's names and words from their reading, e.g. *dinosaur, family, dinner, children.* Extend to written forms and note syllable boundary in speech and writing

2: 2: T8: to read own poems aloud

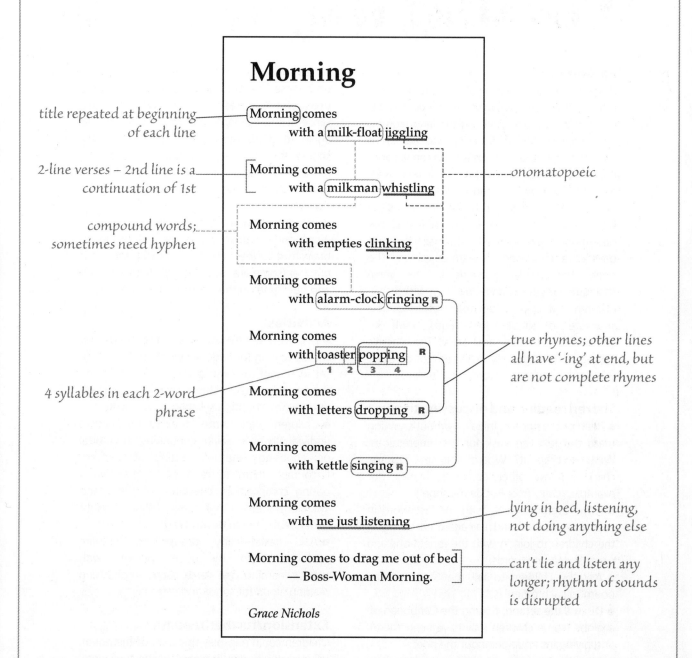

Morning

title repeated at beginning of each line

Morning comes
   with a milk-float jiggling

2-line verses – 2nd line is a continuation of 1st

Morning comes
   with a milkman whistling

— *onomatopoeic*

compound words; sometimes need hyphen

Morning comes
   with empties clinking

Morning comes
   with alarm-clock ringing ʀ

Morning comes
   with toaster popping ʀ
       1   2   3   4

true rhymes; other lines all have '-ing' at end, but are not complete rhymes

4 syllables in each 2-word phrase

Morning comes
   with letters dropping ʀ

Morning comes
   with kettle singing ʀ

Morning comes
   with me just listening

lying in bed, listening, not doing anything else

Morning comes to drag me out of bed
   — Boss-Woman Morning.

can't lie and listen any longer; rhythm of sounds is disrupted

Grace Nichols

2: 2: T9: to identify and discuss patterns of rhythm, rhyme and other features of sound in different poems

2: 2: T10: to comment on and recognise when the reading aloud of a poem makes sense and is effective

2: 2: T15: to use structures from poems as a basis for writing, by extending or substituting elements, inventing own lines, verses; to make class collections, illustrate with captions; to write own poems from initial jottings and words

Caribbean Counting Rhyme

by Pamela Mordecai

Background

Pamela Mordecai is a Jamaican, now living in Canada. She has published many poems for children set in, and reflecting the language of, her childhood. Most cultures have a tradition of counting rhymes and this is a Jamaican version. It also has echoes of Noah and his ark – animals marching two by two (and the rhythms of the poem perhaps suggest this). The poem tells the story of a day's fishing by the sea, and the descriptions give a feel for the lazy summer days of a childhood in warmer climes. The poem has regular patterns in the verse structure, rhythms and rhymes, which the children can enjoy when reading aloud. The structure is simple and lends itself to compositions in the same style. The poem's setting encourages the children to consider ways of life in other cultures.

Shared reading and discussing the text

● Read out the poem, initially without showing them the text, and ask for first impressions. What is it about? Where is it set? Do the children know other counting rhymes (for example, 'One, Two, Buckle my shoe')?
● Now reveal the text, with the last word in each verse covered, and read again, encouraging the children to join in with the repetitions and suggest rhyming words.
● Ask the children to tell the 'story' of the poem to each other.
● Discuss the setting, finding the Caribbean on a globe (some children may have been there), and giving information about the poet.
● Read the poem to the children again, asking them to close their eyes and picture the scene, and then use words and phrases to describe it and their feelings.
● Ask the children to consider the structure of the poem. Draw out the four-line verses, the repeated lines, the two-line 'word pictures' with a rhyme at the end.
● Read verse 1 again (the children just listening); clap and count the syllables, noting the number in each line. Repeat for other verses. Note particularly that lines 3 and 4 of each verse have a total of 7 syllables, but split between the 2 lines in different ways, to make sense of the reading. Read some of the verses again to demonstrate how these two lines should flow as one, but noting the pauses required after lines 1 and 2. Note that *seven* has to be read almost as a single syllable to fit the rhythm.
● Ask the children to highlight the rhyming words and explore the spellings. Ask groups to brainstorm other rhyming words for each number (some are more difficult than others!), and put these on the board for later use.

Activities

● Discuss new settings for a similar poem. Use shared writing to model a new verse (or more), set in school for example, using some of the rhymes suggested. 'Think aloud' to focus on the rhythm, counting syllables as you write.
● Children can write their own poems (individually or in pairs), continuing the model or choosing another setting if desired. Encourage them to read each verse aloud during composition, checking for sense and syllable patterns. More able children might continue the poem beyond ten.
● Ask mixed-ability groups to prepare performances of the poem, perhaps with groups learning one verse each, emphasising reading aloud for sense and effect.

Extension/further reading

Children could role-play the story of the poem, using dialogue drawn from clues in the poem. Children can compare the setting with that of their own poems, considering the effect created by different settings. Read other poems by Caribbean poets, such as in *Sunsong* edited by Pamela Mordecai (Longman), *A Caribbean Dozen* edited by John Agard and Grace Nichols (Walker Books), *Down by the River* compiled by Grace Hallworth, (Longman). *Mango Spice* edited by Yvonne Connolly (Black) is a collection of Caribbean songs.

2: 2: W5: to discriminate, orally, syllables in multi-syllabic words using children's names and words from their reading, e.g. *dinosaur, family, dinner, children*. Extend to written forms and note syllable boundary in speech and writing

2: 2: W6: to read on sight and spell all the words from Appendix List 1

2: 2: T5: to discuss story settings: to compare differences; to locate key words and phrases in text; to consider how different settings influence events and behaviour

significance of setting: warm, sunny, seaside

repeated lines

no pause between lines 3 and 4; should flow

rhyming words have different spellings

7 syllables between lines 3 and 4 (in different combinations)

perhaps these fish can 'walk' across wet sand using their fins

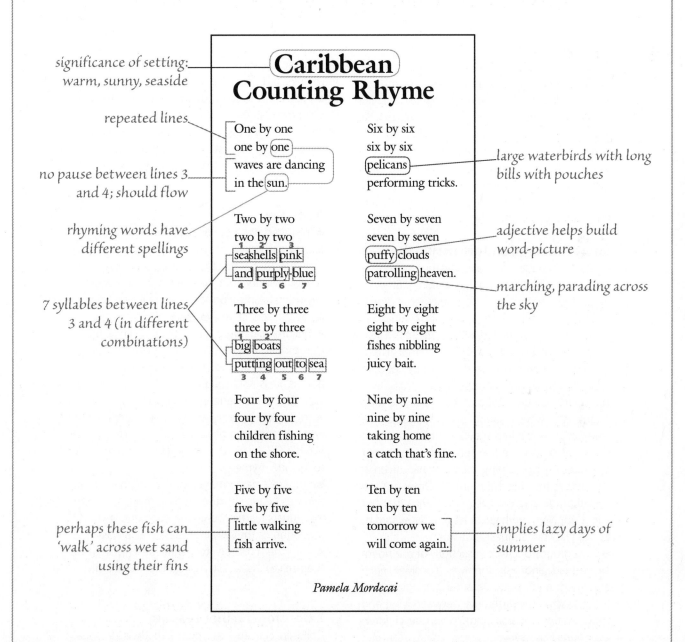

Caribbean Counting Rhyme

One by one
one by one
waves are dancing
in the sun.

Two by two
two by two
seashells pink
and purply-blue

Three by three
three by three
big boats
putting out to sea

Four by four
four by four
children fishing
on the shore.

Five by five
five by five
little walking
fish arrive.

Six by six
six by six
pelicans
performing tricks.

Seven by seven
seven by seven
puffy clouds
patrolling heaven.

Eight by eight
eight by eight
fishes nibbling
juicy bait.

Nine by nine
nine by nine
taking home
a catch that's fine.

Ten by ten
ten by ten
tomorrow we
will come again.

Pamela Mordecai

large waterbirds with long bills with pouches

adjective helps build word-picture

marching, parading across the sky

implies lazy days of summer

2: 2: T9: to identify and discuss patterns of rhythm, rhyme and other features of sound in different poems

2: 2: T10: to comment on and recognise when the reading aloud of a poem makes sense and is effective

2: 2: T15: to use structures from poems as a basis for writing, by extending or substituting elements, inventing own lines, verses; to make class collections, illustrate with captions; to write own poems from initial jottings and words

Word of a Lie

by Jackie Kay

Background

Jackie Kay is a black Scottish poet and many of her poems reflect the difficulties of a mixed-race childhood. This poem suggests a child feeling insecure and needing to impress, a feeling with which many of the children will identify. They will enjoy reading the boasts (all set in the real world of childhood) and discussing the differences between reality and fantasy, and sorting the possible from the impossible and improbable.

Shared reading and discussing the text

● Cover the title and read the poem (in the voice of a child), giving the children time to enjoy the humour. Ask for first impressions. What is it about? Who is speaking? What do they think the repeated phrase means? Have they heard it used before? Explain that it is a colloquial expression used by some people when telling an unbelievable story.

● Ask the children what they think the title might be. After sharing some suggestions, reveal it. The children may be surprised that it does not reflect the line repeated throughout the poem. Discuss why the poet has given it this title. Is the child lying or not? Draw out the idea that, despite the child's insistence that he/she is not lying, perhaps most of what is said is, as the last lines suggest, not true.

● Give groups of children sections of the poem to re-read and ask them to consider each statement and decide whether it is possible or likely. Discuss the difference between lying and exaggerating (or boasting). Have the children ever done this? Why?

● Note that the repeated phrase is in capitals and on a separate line for emphasis. Note the absence of full stops, and demonstrate by reading aloud, where pauses are needed. Where would full stops go?

● Highlight the commas used to separate ideas in a list. Model a sentence about yourself to demonstrate this use of commas: *I have brown hair, blue eyes, freckles and glasses.*

● Explore the rhymes, asking the children to look at sections of the poem. Highlight the rhymes and note their position.

● Focus on the last four lines, clearly separated from the rest, emphasising how the pattern has changed. Is the last statement a lie or the truth? Refer back to the last few lines of the main part, noting the more serious tone. Is this a lie as well?

Activities

● In shared writing, consider some new lines to add to the poem. Ask the children to suggest activities that they take part in, at home or at school. Model four new lines for the poem, using the same format. The children should enjoy the licence to exaggerate!

● Children can write their own new lines, using the model above, then role-play dialogues, taking turns to read the lines from their own poems. Less able children can work in a group with support to generate ideas. A writing frame with the key phrases will support independent writing, for example *I can... and that's NO WORD OF A LIE.* More able children might try to include rhymes.

● Prepare a performance of the original poem, perhaps taking short sections in groups, or with individuals learning one line each and a choral rendering of the refrain. Evaluate as a class.

● Ask the children to write descriptions of themselves as a list, using the model given earlier.

Extension/further reading

Children can add the poem to their personal anthologies. Encourage them to write about the poem, its ideas and structure, and explain their personal responses. Read other poems by Jackie Kay; compare them and express preferences. See her collections *The Frog Who Dreamed She Was an Opera Singer* (Bloomsbury) and *Three Has Gone* (Puffin). Jackie Kay poems also appear in *Five Finger-Piglets*, edited by Brian Patten (Macmillan).

2: 2: S8: to use commas to separate items in a list

2: 2: T8: to read own poems aloud

2: 2: T10: to comment on and recognise when the reading aloud of a poem makes sense and is effective

title is not the same as refrain; raises the question – lying or not?

colloquial expression repeated throughout

capitals and a separate line for emphasis

impossible/unlikely

possible

more serious; are these statements true?

same format as NO WORD OF A LIE

is this the only true statement of the poem? or is it a lie as well?

Word of a Lie

I am the fastest runner in my school and that's
NO WORD OF A LIE
I've got gold fillings in my teeth and that's
NO WORD OF A LIE
In my garden, I've got my own big bull and that's
NO WORD OF A LIE
I'm brilliant at giving my enemies grief and that's
NO WORD OF A LIE
I can multiply three billion and twenty-seven by nine billion four
   thousand and one in two seconds and that's
NO WORD OF A LIE
I can calculate the distance between planets before you've had
toast and that's
NO WORD OF A LIE
I can always tell when my best pals boast and that's
NO WORD OF A LIE
I'd been round the world twice before I was three and a quarter
   and that's
NO WORD OF A LIE
I am definitely my mother's favourite daughter and that's
NO WORD OF A LIE
I am brilliant at fake laughter, I go Ha aha Ha ha ha and that's
NO WORD OF A LIE
I can tell the weather from one look at the sky and that's
NO WORD OF A LIE
I can predict disasters, floods, earthquakes and murders and that's
NO WORD OF A LIE
I can always tell when other people lie and that's
NO WORD OF A LIE
I can even tell if someone is going to die and that's
NO WORD OF A LIE
I am the most popular girl in my entire school and that's
NO WORD OF A LIE
I know the golden rule, don't play the fool, don't boast, be shy and
   that's
NO WORD OF A LIE
I am sensitive, I listen, I have kind brown eyes and that's
NO WORD OF A LIE

You don't believe me do you?
ALL RIGHT, ALL RIGHT, ALL RIGHT
I am the biggest liar in my school and that's
NO WORD OF A LIE

Jackie Kay

not a regular rhyme scheme; rhymes for the sake of it perhaps

used in order to rhyme with 'daughter'; different spelling, same sound

same spelling; different sound

commas used to separate items in a list

gap to emphasise concluding ideas that follow

makes everything else a lie

2: 2: T11: to identify and discuss favourite poems and poets, using appropriate terms (poet, poem, verse, rhyme, etc.) and referring to the language of the poems

2: 2: T15: to use structures from poems as a basis for writing, by extending or substituting elements, inventing own lines, verses; to make class collections, illustrate with captions; to write own poems from initial jottings and words

Conversation

by Michael Rosen

Background

Michael Rosen is one of our best-known children's poets. His poetry explores childhood experiences – friends, family, school – often in the spoken language of children. Much of it is drawn from observations of his own five children. 'Conversation' explores a very familiar situation – the child who cannot stop asking why! It is a poem for two voices – parent and child – and reflects the frustration of the adult who runs out of answers (because the questions are unanswerable). The language and structure are simple and patterned; the conversation and repeated words providing a structuring device that offers an accessible model for the children's own writing.

Shared reading and discussing the text

● Conceal the title and read the poem with the children, emphasising through expression the fact that it is a dialogue. Ask the children who is speaking in the poem. Does the poem present a familiar situation?

● Discuss what the title might be, then reveal it. Do the children think this is a good title for the poem? Are the people in the poem *really* having a conversation?

● Give out copies of the poem and ask pairs of children to highlight the speakers' lines in two different colours. Notice the pattern through most of the poem, but the change at the end, where two lines are spoken by the adult. Re-read the last few lines again if necessary.

● Re-read the poem, with half the class taking each part, or in pairs.

● Consider the adult's response each time. Are they reasonable answers to the question *Why?* Note that after *Because it's summer,* there is no longer a reasonable answer to give. Do the children have experience of adults responding like this? (*Just because* or *Because I say so.*)

● Ask the children to consider why the penultimate line is hyphenated. Refer to *Tea-time* in the previous line, and link to other such phrases such as *lunch-time, play-time, high-time-you-...-time.*

● Discuss *What?* in the last line.

● Focus on the spelling of *why* – notice the *wh* digraph (silent 'h'). Ask the children to discuss other words beginning with *w.* Categorise them into *w* and *wh* spellings. Draw particular attention to the 'question' words (for example, *what* and *when* in the text).

Activities

● Ask two children to read the poem again. Draw two figures on the board (adult and child) and use speech bubbles to record the first exchange. Ask the children to do the same for the next pair of lines. Demonstrate how to turn this into dialogue, first adding speech marks to the text, and then introducing *said Mum/ George.*

● Model a similar conversation, with a child contributing the *Why?*, in a different situation (*I'm just going to the shop/upstairs*). In shared writing, record the beginning of the dialogue in the style of the poem. Consider how the adult might end the conversation (*school-time, bed-time*). In pairs, children can plan and role-play a similar conversation. They can then write it in the same form as the poem.

● Ask the children to add speech marks to the text (the original or their own), and then add the narrative links (*said Mum*). Act as scribe for less able children's 'conversations', using shared writing to add speech marks. More able children can consider alternatives to 'said'.

● Children could make a comic strip of the conversation, using speech bubbles.

Extension/further reading

Share other Michael Rosen poems. Compile a class book of his poems (or a display for 'poet of the week'). Compare the poems and express preferences, referring to the subject matter, format and favourite words or phrases. Other 'conversation' poems include: 'The Dark Avenger, for Two Voices' by Trevor Millum (owner and dog!), 'Conversation Piece' by Gareth Owen (teacher and child) – both in *The Works* (Macmillan).

2: 2: W3: to read and spell words containing the digraph *'wh'*, *'ph'*, *'ch'* (as in *Christopher*)

2: 2: S6: to identify speech marks in reading, understand their purpose, use the terms correctly

2: 2: T8: to read own poems aloud

so for at least two voices

two speakers: adult and child

'wh' digraph

begins all answers

losing patience, turning 'why' back to the child

distraction, trying to end the conversation

hyphenated like tea-time

not 'why?'; child confused by previous answer

Conversation

I'm just going out for a moment.
Why?
To make a cup of tea.
Why?
Because I'm thirsty.
Why?
Because it's hot.
Why?
Because the sun is shining.
Why?
Because it's summer.
Why?
Because that's when it is.
Why?
Why don't you stop saying why?
Why?
Tea-time. That's why.
High-time-you-stopped-saying-why-time.
What?

Michael Rosen

2: 2: T11: to identify and discuss favourite poems and poets, using appropriate terms (poet, poem, verse, rhyme, etc.) and referring to the language of the poems

2: 2: T15: to use structures from poems as a basis for writing, by extending or substituting elements, inventing own lines, verses; to make class collections, illustrate with captions; to write own poems from initial jottings and words

Dictionary entries

Background

This extract from a children's dictionary demonstrates many of the features common to such texts. Headwords are clearly identified in bold, as are related words where included. Each entry identifies the word class and gives other forms of the word, such as verbs, and comparatives and superlatives of adjectives. Definitions are simple and are expressed using the word itself, illustrating its use in a sentence. This extract contains words formed using the prefix *un*, allowing the children to explore ways of forming negatives and antonyms.

Shared reading and discussing the text

● If possible, have a range of dictionaries on display.

● Show the text to the children and ask them what kind of book it comes from and how they know. Ask what dictionaries are for (looking up spellings and meanings of words). Ask how they are organised. What letter do all these words begin with?

● Sing and recite the alphabet to revise alphabetical order. Reinforce this by asking for the letter before/after another. Where in the alphabet is *u*?

● Identify significant visual features on the page – bold type, small capitals, different sizes.

● Read the first entry and focus on each part: first word – the headword, what you are looking up (for spelling or meaning); the definition – tells you what the word means; demonstrate by tying and untying a shoelace for example; *word class* (in small capitals) – this shows what kind of word it is (explain at an appropriate level – for example, verb = *an action word*); the verb or adjective forms – put each in a sentence to demonstrate that they all mean the same thing, but we use them in different ways in different sentences.

● Repeat for the second entry, asking the children to put the word (in different tenses) into sentences.

● Now read the entry for *unhappy*, explaining the uses of adjectives, comparative, superlative, and adverb, putting each in a sentence to illustrate. (Children do not need to remember the word classes; the purpose is to show the information that dictionaries commonly contain. The focus is the headword and definition; avoid over-focusing on word class.)

● Highlight *un* in each word, noting that each headword begins with this. Read the first entry again and note that it is made up of *un* and *do*. Demonstrate with shoelaces again – show how *undo* is the opposite of *do*. Give the children copies of the text and ask them to highlight in different colours the two parts of each word (*un* + root word).

● Focus on one or two more words (*unfair, unhappy* perhaps) to demonstrate that the *un* prefix also makes opposites here. Now ask the children to read each headword without its prefix *un* and write these on the board. Demonstrate that these parts of the words are in alphabetical order.

Activities

● Give the children lists of words to put into alphabetical order by initial letter (using names or topic words, for example). Less able children may need words with initial letters that follow each other in direct sequence alphabetically (for example, *apple, bread, chips…*). More able children may be able to order by second letter.

● Give pairs simple words for which to write definitions. They can read out their definitions for others to work out what the words are.

● Ask the children to make opposites of given words by adding *un* (*kind, lucky, safe, tidy*). They should then write definitions for each word. More able children might explore other ways of making opposites – by adding a different prefix (*dis – appear, agree*) or with a different word (*bad/good, big/small*).

Extension/further reading

Children could compete in pairs to find words in the dictionary as quickly as possible. Explore a range of dictionaries to find out what other information they contain.

Dictionary entries

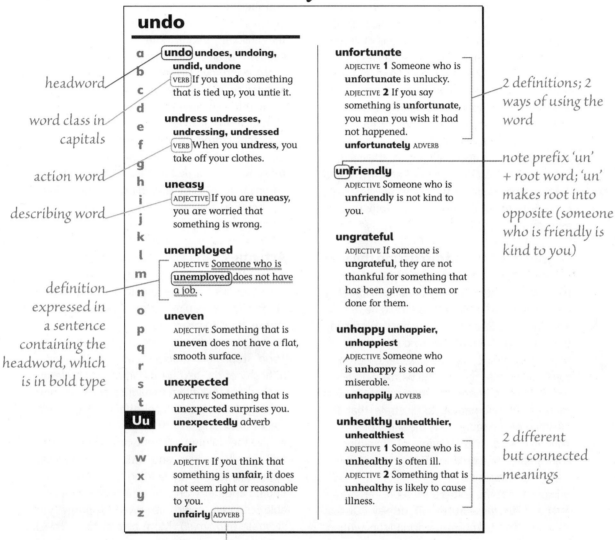

undo

headword

word class in capitals

action word

describing word

definition expressed in a sentence containing the headword, which is in bold type

a | b | c | d | e | f | g | h | i | j | k | l | m | n | o | p | q | r | s | t | **Uu** | v | w | x | y | z

undo undoes, undoing, undid, undone
VERB If you **undo** something that is tied up, you untie it.

undress undresses, undressing, undressed
VERB When you **undress**, you take off your clothes.

uneasy
ADJECTIVE If you are **uneasy**, you are worried that something is wrong.

unemployed
ADJECTIVE Someone who is **unemployed** does not have a job.

uneven
ADJECTIVE Something that is **uneven** does not have a flat, smooth surface.

unexpected
ADJECTIVE Something that is **unexpected** surprises you.
unexpectedly adverb

unfair
ADJECTIVE If you think that something is **unfair**, it does not seem right or reasonable to you.
unfairly ADVERB

unfortunate
ADJECTIVE **1** Someone who is **unfortunate** is unlucky.
ADJECTIVE **2** If you say something is **unfortunate**, you mean you wish it had not happened.
unfortunately ADVERB

unfriendly
ADJECTIVE Someone who is **unfriendly** is not kind to you.

ungrateful
ADJECTIVE If someone is **ungrateful**, they are not thankful for something that has been given to them or done for them.

unhappy unhappier, unhappiest
ADJECTIVE Someone who is **unhappy** is sad or miserable.
unhappily ADVERB

unhealthy unhealthier, unhealthiest
ADJECTIVE **1** Someone who is **unhealthy** is often ill.
ADJECTIVE **2** Something that is **unhealthy** is likely to cause illness.

2 definitions; 2 ways of using the word

note prefix 'un' + root word; 'un' makes root into opposite (someone who is friendly is kind to you)

2 different but connected meanings

a different word class; used to show how something is done or happens

Synonyms

Background

This thesaurus extract introduces the children to another alphabetically ordered text. It lists some of the words most overused in children's writing, and suggests alternatives. The synonyms are in some cases used with nouns to illustrate the shades of meaning in those words. The children should understand the purpose and use of a thesaurus as a tool for improving their writing through a wider vocabulary. Through learning about synonyms, the children can also develop knowledge of antonyms, and links can be made to the dictionary text (see page 66), where the use of the prefix *un* was explored.

Shared reading and discussing the text

● Display a range of dictionaries and thesauruses.
● Show the children the text, and ask what they think it is and what its purpose could be.
● Read the title and introduction, reinforcing the look and sound of the word *synonyms*.
● Read the first entry and ask the children to consider the meanings of the words. Suggest a sentence using *angry* and then replace it with each of the alternatives to illustrate that the meaning of the sentence is the same or similar. You might discuss shades of meaning if appropriate. (*I was angry/furious… at being left out of the team.*)
● Explain that the text is a *thesaurus* and draw attention to thesauruses on display. Discuss their use and purpose, particularly in writing. Like the dictionary, it is a *reference* text, to be consulted when needed.
● Highlight the headwords (noting the bold type), and ask the children to consider the order – reminding them of earlier work on alphabetical order.
● Read the next entry. Ask the children to read each phrase and then replace *bad* with the alternatives. Note that *bad* can be used in lots of different ways and that the suggested words make the meaning more precise (a *naughty* child or a *spiteful* child?). Refer to a dictionary if they are unfamiliar with any of the words.

● Read the rest of the text, focusing on sounds and spellings, replacing words with alternatives, and discussing meaning and effect. Some of the children might note that some of the headwords also have similar meanings – *bad/ nasty, good/lovely/nice.*
● Refer to the dictionary text (see page 66). Remind the children that the words in that text all had the prefix *un*, which made words into opposites. Introduce the word *antonym*, writing it on the board and comparing with *synonym*.
● Focus on *happy* in this text, noting its antonym, formed by adding *un*. Generate other examples – *unkind, (un)helpful, (un)friendly, unpleasant.*

Activities

● Give the children copies of the text, cut up into sections, to reassemble in alphabetical order. Give less able children the alphabet cut into sections to order first.
● Give the children a piece of text with *nice* or *good* repeated (differentiate the reading difficulty of the text for different reading levels of children). Ask them to rewrite it, substituting synonyms. Compare the effect of the two pieces of writing.
● Give the children a list of words (for example, *tall, small, heavy*) and ask them to find opposites, either by adding a prefix or by finding another word, and illustrate them. Less able children could be given opposites to illustrate (*big/small*). More able children could put the antonyms into sentences to demonstrate their meanings, and illustrate those.

Extension/further reading

Children could explore synonyms for *said* to be used in their writing, and role-play dialogues to illustrate the effect of these choices. Explore a range of thesauruses, noting how they are organised and laid out. The children could make a poster for the classroom about thesauruses and how to use them. Using a range of thesauruses, ask the children to find synonyms for other words.

2: 2: W8: to spell words with common prefixes, e.g. *'un'*, *'dis'*, to indicate the negative

2: 2: W11: the use of antonyms: collect, discuss differences of meaning and their spelling

Synonyms

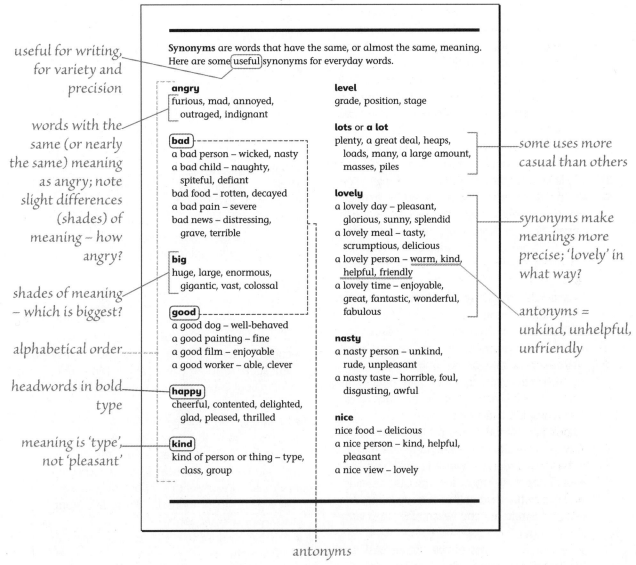

useful for writing, for variety and precision

words with the same (or nearly the same) meaning as angry; note slight differences (shades) of meaning – how angry?

shades of meaning – which is biggest?

alphabetical order

headwords in bold type

meaning is 'type', not 'pleasant'

Synonyms are words that have the same, or almost the same, meaning. Here are some useful synonyms for everyday words.

angry
furious, mad, annoyed, outraged, indignant

bad
a bad person – wicked, nasty
a bad child – naughty, spiteful, defiant
bad food – rotten, decayed
a bad pain – severe
bad news – distressing, grave, terrible

big
huge, large, enormous, gigantic, vast, colossal

good
a good dog – well-behaved
a good painting – fine
a good film – enjoyable
a good worker – able, clever

happy
cheerful, contented, delighted, glad, pleased, thrilled

kind
kind of person or thing – type, class, group

level
grade, position, stage

lots or **a lot**
plenty, a great deal, heaps, loads, many, a large amount, masses, piles

lovely
a lovely day – pleasant, glorious, sunny, splendid
a lovely meal – tasty, scrumptious, delicious
a lovely person – warm, kind, helpful, friendly
a lovely time – enjoyable, great, fantastic, wonderful, fabulous

nasty
a nasty person – unkind, rude, unpleasant
a nasty taste – horrible, foul, disgusting, awful

nice
nice food – delicious
a nice person – kind, helpful, pleasant
a nice view – lovely

some uses more casual than others

synonyms make meanings more precise; 'lovely' in what way?

antonyms = unkind, unhelpful, unfriendly

antonyms

2: 2: T18: to use other alphabetically ordered texts, e.g. indexes, directories, listings, registers; to discuss how they are used

Glossary and Index

Extracts 1 and 2

Background

Glossaries and indexes are further examples of alphabetically ordered texts, often found in non-fiction books. A glossary gives a definition or further information about vocabulary in a text, and an index allows a reader to find specific topics. Children need to be taught the use and purpose of glossaries and indexes to help them access and understand texts about topics of interest. This glossary and index are from a book about butterflies and moths and are linked to the next text, an explanation about the life cycle of the butterfly. The extracts allow the children to further their knowledge of alphabetically ordered texts and to understand how they are used, in conjunction with the explanatory text.

Shared reading and discussing the text

● If possible, display a range of information books that include glossaries and indexes.

● Show the glossary to the children and ask if they know what it is and what it might be used for. Read the title together and discuss its meaning, explaining that a glossary gives definitions, like a dictionary.

● Look at how the text is presented, referring to work on dictionaries – noting the list format, alphabetical order and words in bold type.

● Read the first entry and discuss meaning, drawing on the children's prior knowledge, and using illustrations and examples to clarify terminology.

● Repeat for the rest of the entries. Ask the children if they know what kind of book the glossary might be in. What is the subject? Note that the headwords are technical terms for features related to the topic of the book (in this case butterflies and moths).

● Now look at the second text (the index). Discuss its use and purpose, demonstrating in other books if possible (and comparing with a contents page if appropriate). Highlight the alphabetical order again, noting that words beginning with the same letter are grouped for easier identification.

● Draw attention to the fact that most of the words in the glossary are also in the index, noting that they are from the same non-fiction book.

● Read some of the entries, discussing the words and numbers, noting commas to separate the list of page numbers. Demonstrate possible confusion if commas were omitted. Note particularly entries such as *caterpillars 16–21*, which shows that a whole section is about caterpillars.

● Look at the entry for *feelers*, explaining that *see* (in italic to differentiate the word function) refers you to another entry (*antennae*). Look back to the glossary, noting that *feelers* is another word for *antennae*.

Activities

● Give the children copies of the glossary and the index, cut into sections, to reassemble into alphabetical order. Provide most children with sections of text to order by initial letter only (with support for the less able). More able children could use individual entries to order by second or third letter.

● Children can make illustrated personal glossaries from this text, for use within a science topic. Use selected entries for spelling and handwriting practice. Less able children may need to work with support, or in mixed-ability pairs, to produce an illustrated group glossary of selected terms.

● Ask the children to match glossary items to entries in the index, noting pages on which each would be found. More able children might also match glossary entries to their definitions (using dictionaries or other resources if needed).

● Give the children cards with words from the glossary and/or the index. The children can compete in pairs to find the entry first, reading out the definition/page numbers.

Extension/further reading

Make class and personal glossaries relating to other curriculum topics as they arise.

2: 2: T16: to use dictionaries and glossaries to locate words by using initial letter

2: 2: T17: that dictionaries and glossaries give definitions and explanations; discuss what definitions are, explore some simple definitions in dictionaries

headings in large and bold print

Glossary

all these words are from the book and are here to provide further information

headwords (bold)

the young form of an insect

antennae The feelers on an insect's head.

camouflage How an animal uses its colours to hide.

caterpillar The larva of a butterfly or moth.

cocoon A silk case made by a caterpillar.

insect An animal with six legs and three parts to its body.

metamorphosis When a young insect changes into an adult insect.

bees make this into honey

nectar Sugary liquid made by flowers.

poisonous Harmful.

pollination When an animal carries pollen from one flower to another. The flower can then make seeds.

proboscis The feeding tube on the head of an insect.

pupa A hard case made from the skin of a larva.

scale A tiny flake on the wing of a butterfly or moth.

shed To get rid of something naturally, such as skin or hair.

shimmer To shine with moving light.

alphabetical order continues in 2nd column

dust-like grains that can fertilise another flower

technical vocabulary which is likely to be unfamiliar; topic-specific

Index

grouped by initial letter, ordered by 2nd/3rd letter

denotes a long section about the item

antennae 4, 5, 7, 31

camouflage 26, 27, 31
caterpillars 16–21, 22, 24, 25, 26, 28, 31
cocoon 22, 23, 31
colours 6, 7, 8, 9, 24, 26, 27

eggs 16–17
eye-spots 9, 24

feelers *see* antennae
flowers 12, 14, 15, 22

flying 6, 10–11, 14, 29
food 12–15, 18–19, 28, 29

jaws 16

leaves 16, 17, 18, 19, 26, 29
legs 4, 16

metamorphosis 21, 31

nectar 11, 12, 13, 14, 22, 28, 31

plants 16, 18, 26, 28
poisonous 24, 31
pollen 22
pollination 22, 31
proboscis 12, 13, 14, 31
pupa 20–21, 22, 31

scales 8, 31
shedding 18, 19, 20
silk 22, 23
skin 18, 19, 20

wings 4, 6, 7, 8–9, 10, 14, 20, 21, 23, 26, 27

commas to separate lists of page numbers; could cause confusion without

2: 2: T18: to use other alphabetically ordered texts, e.g. indexes, directories, listings, registers; to discuss how they are used

2: 2: T20: to make class dictionaries and glossaries of special interest words, giving explanations and definitions, e.g. linked to topics, derived from stories, poems

2: 2: W10: new words from reading linked to particular topics, to build individual collections of personal interest or significant words

Butterflies and Moths

Background

This is an explanatory text, which describes the life cycle of butterflies (and moths). It can be linked to the previous text – a glossary and index from the same book. The children can use the glossary to find definitions of words from this text. There are presentational features common to this type of text, including headings, sub-headings and bold print.

Shared reading and discussing the text

● Read the title and refer to the previous extract, noting that this is on the same topic.
● Ask the children why some of the words are in large and/or bold print. Draw out the eye-catching effect to draw attention to important parts of the text and to add interest. Consider the purpose of the sub-headings. Note the words in bold type within the text, and demonstrate that these words are defined in the glossary – see the previous text.
● Read the text with the children, reminding them of the use of syllabification to read multi-syllabic words. Ask them to explain, in their own words, what the text is about. Draw out that the text *explains* the life cycle of a butterfly (or moth). (Make links to any previous experience of growth and change.)
● Read the first sub-heading again, and ask the children what this section of text is about. Read the section and ask the children in pairs to identify three or four key words that tell us about this stage of the cycle. Make a class list to include, for example *butterflies*, *eggs, hatch, caterpillars*. Note that sentences 3, 4 and 5 add information about caterpillars to help the reader understand what a caterpillar is. Repeat for the other sections, identifying key words and phrases from each, and noting supplementary information.

Activities

● Put enlarged pictures from the text on the board and ask the children to sequence them. Model writing simple captions for the first two, drawing on the word bank. (Write captions on pieces of paper to allow reordering later.) Re-read each sentence as it is written, to check for sense and punctuation. Comment on the verb tenses, occasionally making deliberate mistakes.
● Ask the children to discuss in pairs what the next caption (sentence) should be, drawing on words from the second section. Share ideas and write the next caption. Continue until the cycle is complete (5 or 6 sentences).
● Add arrows between each set of pictures and captions to reinforce that this is a sequence of steps that always happen in the same order. Ask the children to consider what happens to the butterfly next. Draw out that it will lay eggs, so the cycle will continue. Rearrange the pictures and captions in a circle to demonstrate this, using arrows to indicate the sequence.
● Give the children cut-up copies of the text to match pictures to text.
● Prepare copies of the shared writing – the pictures and captions – for the children to reassemble, or with gaps to fill.
● Children can compile their own glossaries from this text, using the glossary from the previous text and adding to it using dictionaries and other resources.
● More able children can draw and label their own cyclical diagrams, from the model, or make large copies for classroom reference.

Extension/further reading

If the complete text is available, the children can find out more about butterflies, first generating a list of questions, such as *What do butterflies eat?* Encourage use of the contents, glossary and index. Children can draw cyclical diagrams to explain other similar processes (such as the life cycle of a frog). Children could read *The Very Hungry Caterpillar* by Eric Carle (Puffin). For more information on the butterfly's (and other insects') life cycle, see *Eyewitness – Butterfly and Moth; Insect; Amphibian* (Dorling Kindersley), *Amazing Insects* (Collins) and *Amazing Worlds – Insects; Amphibians, Reptiles and Fish* (Dorling Kindersley).

2: 2: W10: new words from reading linked to particular topics, to build individual collections of personal interest or significant words

2: 2: S7: to investigate and recognise a range of other ways of presenting texts, e.g. speech bubbles, enlarged, bold or italicised print, captions, headings and sub-headings

heading in enlarged and bold print

sub-headings in bold

syllabification for reading

indicates an entry in the glossary (previous text)

Butterflies and Moths

Eggs and caterpillars

Butterflies and moths lay their eggs on plants. The eggs hatch into **caterpillars.** A caterpillar looks a bit like a worm. It has three pairs of legs and four pairs of suckers. The legs and suckers help the caterpillar to grip the leaves and stems of plants.

supplementary information to aid understanding

Caterpillar food

Caterpillars start eating as soon as they hatch. They only like certain kinds of leaves. A caterpillar eats all day. It grows so large that its skin gets tight. Then it has to **shed** the old skin and grow a larger one. Sometimes, caterpillars can kill a plant by eating all its leaves.

illustrations help explain text

sub-heading as question implies section will answer question

What is a pupa?

When a caterpillar is fully grown, it stops eating and sheds its skin for the last time. Lying under the old skin is a **pupa.** A pupa is a hard case made from the skin of the caterpillar.

Inside the pupa, the caterpillar slowly changes into an adult butterfly. This is called **metamorphosis.** It means changing shape. Then the pupa splits open and the new adult butterfly comes out.

2: 2: T19: to read flow charts and cyclical diagrams that explain a process

2: 2: T20: to make class dictionaries and glossaries of special interest words, giving explanations and definitions, e.g. linked to topics, derived from stories, poems

2: 2: T21: to produce simple flow charts or diagrams that explain a process

How flowers grow

Background

This text explains the life cycle of flowering plants, and links well with science topics on plants and growth. The stages of the cycle are explained in simple language, while introducing key terms related to the topic. The text has an introductory paragraph and further information to extend understanding of the process. The children will be able to identify the key steps in the process and represent these as a cyclical diagram. It further develops the children's understanding of explanatory texts, building on the previous extract.

Shared reading and discussing the text

● Read the title and ask the children what kind of text they think this is.

● Read the complete text and ask the children to explain what it is about. Draw out that is an explanation of how plants grow from seeds (referring, if appropriate, to the previous extract about the life cycle of a butterfly).

● Highlight technical vocabulary within the text, and ask the children how they might find out the meaning of unfamiliar words – suggest dictionaries, and remind them of the glossary studied earlier. They might also note that the diagram can help. Discuss the labels, which identify and name important parts of the plant. Ask the children to note particularly the size of the seed (tinier than a pinhead!). You could discuss *fruit* here, which may be different from their everyday understanding of the word.

● Read the first section again. Note that this is an introduction, which gives background information about how plants grow.

● Read the sequenced steps one at a time and ask pairs to draw each stage as you read it. You might also draw the pictures, on separate pieces of paper, modelling how to label them.

● Cover the boxed section *How seeds are spread*. Ask the children what happens. How do the seeds get from inside the flowers to the ground so that they can grow into new plants?

● Read the section. Add another picture to complete the process, choosing one of the options. Add arrows to the pictures to indicate the sequence. What happens next? Draw an arrow going from the last picture back to the first to indicate that the cycle begins again. Rearrange your pictures to demonstrate the cycle. 'Read' your diagram to the children.

Activities

● Ask the children to 'read' their pictures to each other.

● Children can now redraw the pictures as a cyclical diagram, using arrows to show the sequence. Ask them to label their diagrams and write one or two sentences for each picture to explain the process. Encourage more able children to add supplementary information to their diagrams, to make their explanations more detailed. Give less able children labels to match to pictures and to sequence them to produce a complete diagram.

● Ask the children to highlight technical vocabulary in the text. They can then write a glossary (in alphabetical order), using dictionaries and other resources (including the Internet) to write definitions. They can draw on the earlier extract (see page 70) as a model. Give less able children a selected range of words, and definitions to pair with them.

● Use some of the vocabulary from the extract for spelling and handwriting practice.

Extension/further reading

Produce a display (as part of a related topic, perhaps) with a labelled picture of a plant and cyclical diagrams. Use captions to describe the literacy features of the display. Allow the children access to the Internet and non-fiction books to research other information about plants. Ask them to produce cyclical diagrams to explain other life processes in animals and plants. See, for example *Eyewitness Plant* (Dorling Kindersley), *Discovery Guides: World of Plants* (Two-Can Publishing), *Flowers, Fruits and Seeds* by Sally Morgan (Belitha Press) and *Plants: Flowers, Fruits and Seeds* by Angela Royston (Heinemann).

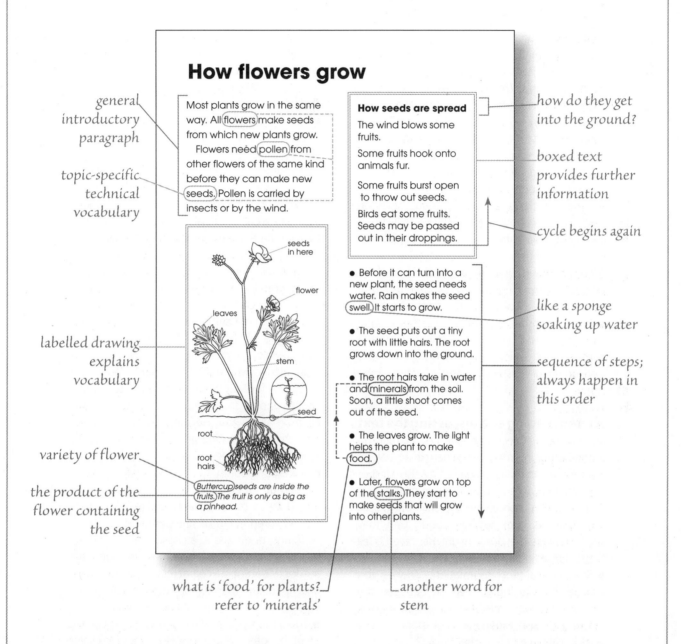

How flowers grow

general introductory paragraph

topic-specific technical vocabulary

Most plants grow in the same way. All flowers make seeds from which new plants grow.
Flowers need pollen from other flowers of the same kind before they can make new seeds. Pollen is carried by insects or by the wind.

How seeds are spread

The wind blows some fruits.

Some fruits hook onto animals fur.

Some fruits burst open to throw out seeds.

Birds eat some fruits. Seeds may be passed out in their droppings.

how do they get into the ground?

boxed text provides further information

cycle begins again

● Before it can turn into a new plant, the seed needs water. Rain makes the seed swell. It starts to grow.

like a sponge soaking up water

● The seed puts out a tiny root with little hairs. The root grows down into the ground.

sequence of steps; always happen in this order

● The root hairs take in water and minerals from the soil. Soon, a little shoot comes out of the seed.

● The leaves grow. The light helps the plant to make food.

● Later, flowers grow on top of the stalks. They start to make seeds that will grow into other plants.

labelled drawing explains vocabulary

seeds in here

flower

leaves

stem

seed

root

root hairs

Buttercup seeds are inside the fruits. The fruit is only as big as a pinhead.

variety of flower

the product of the flower containing the seed

what is 'food' for plants? refer to 'minerals'

another word for stem

Book blurbs

Extracts 1 and 2

Background

Dick King-Smith and Jill Tomlinson are well known for their stories about animals. *The Hodgeheg* and *The Otter Who Wanted to Know*, from which these blurbs are taken, have similar themes, involving young animal characters learning about life and its problems. Looking at the blurbs will encourage awareness of authorship and publication, as well as introducing some of the stories' themes. The settings for the stories are realistic and can teach readers about the difficulties of living in particular environments, as well as suggest parallels with their own lives.

The following three texts, extracts from both books, will allow children to compare different aspects of the books, considering the ways the authors approach themes, settings and characters, and their use of narrative and dialogue. The children can then draw on this developing understanding to write their own stories.

Shared reading and discussing the text

● Read the first section of the first extract (up to the author information). Where in a book do the children think they would find this kind of writing? Introduce or remind them of the term *blurb* and its purpose. Ask the children to sum up what this book will be about. Can they suggest what the book might be called? Tell them, discussing what it might mean.

● Read the author information. Why is this included? (Note the connection between the author's life and the themes of his books, drawing on real experiences for stories.) Why does it list some of his other books?

● Read the second extract. Ask the children what they have learned about this book, urging them to speculate on the title. Why is there no information about the author?

● Ask who writes blurbs. Introduce the role of publishers in producing and selling the book and the need to make it sound attractive.

● Ask the children to discuss what they have learned about the two stories: compare and list the characters, settings and themes. Look for similarities. What have they learned about the characters, Max and Pat?

Activities

● Focus on the author information about Dick King-Smith. Ask a child to tell you something about his/her own life. Report this to the class, using the child's name and in the third person (*George was born on…*). Use shared writing to model your own biography, in the third person, as if you were a publisher. Discuss verb tenses and agreement, sometimes making errors to be corrected. Ask the children to consider what information they would include in a blurb. What would interest a reader?

● Ask the children to write their own life histories, in the same form, for inclusion in a publisher's blurb. To help them write in the third person, they might first tell their biography to a partner, who would then retell it to a third person. A writing frame with sentence starters could support independent writing (*Xxx was born on xxx in Xxx. He/she enjoys xxx*) for less able children. Encourage more able children to consider the reader and what might appeal.

● Ask the children to record what has been learned about each story so far (which will be added to as more extracts are read). Provide the children with a prepared sheet with headings, or discuss as a class initially and draw up an agreed set of headings. Include title, author, setting, characters (names and descriptions), theme (or problem/storyline). Entries can be begun in shared writing.

● The children can discuss and predict what might happen in each story. How does Max solve the problem? What is Pat's *Great Adventure*?

● Ask the children which of the two stories they would most like to read. Put them into small groups, according to preference, and ask them to present an argument to the class, justifying their choice by referring to the information in the blurb. Some children may have read these stories, or others by the same author, and could draw on this.

2: 3: T5: to read about authors from information on book covers, e.g. other books written, whether author is alive or dead, publisher; to become aware of authorship and publication

2: 3: T7: to compare books by different authors on similar themes; to evaluate, giving reasons

Book blurbs

Extract 1

compare; what could it mean?

entices the potential reader

This is the story of Max, the hedgehog who becomes a hodgeheg, who becomes a hero!

setting

The hedgehog family of Number 5A are a happy bunch but they dream of reaching the Park. Unfortunately, a very busy road lies between them and their goal and no one has found a way to cross it in safety. No one, that is, until the determined young Max decides to solve the problem once and for all…

plot summary must not give too much away

leaves questions open; how might he solve problem?

theme – crossing the road is a problem for the hedgehogs

A delightfully original animal adventure from a master storyteller.

describes his character

Dick King-Smith was born near Bristol. After serving in the Grenadier Guards during the Second World War, he spent twenty years as a farmer in Gloucestershire, an experience which inspired many of his stories. He went on to teach at a village primary school. His first book, *The Fox Busters*, was published in 1978. Since then he has written a great number of children's books, including *The Sheep-Pig* (winner of the *Guardian* Award), *Harry's Mad, Noah's Brother, The Hodgeheg, Martin's Mice, Ace, The Cuckoo Child* and many others. He is married with three children and ten grandchildren, and lives in Avon.

author information puts the author into context – makes him seem real

publisher's phrasing – trying to tempt and appeal

he knows about animals and children

Extract 2

setting

Pat is a young sea otter who never stops asking questions – although she doesn't always listen to the answers! Life can be dangerous for a young otter, though, and Pat quickly learns how to deal with hungry sharks and sudden storms. Then, one day, Pat has a Great Adventure – and it is so exciting that she almost forgets to ask any questions!

provides some character information but doesn't give away too much of plot

familiar to young children (link to the poem 'Conversation', see page 64)

theme – learning about danger in her world

Another wonderful character from the author of the very popular *The Owl Who Was Afraid of the Dark.* There are lots more animals to meet in this delightful series by Jill Tomlinson:

The Aardvark Who Wasn't Sure
The Cat Who Wanted to Go Home
The Gorilla Who Wanted to Grow Up

publisher trying to appeal to readers using positive, descriptive words

other animal book – similar titles/themes

2: 3: S2: the need for grammatical agreement, matching verbs to nouns/pronouns, e.g. *I am; the children are;* using simple gender forms, e.g. *his/her* correctly

Story openings
by Dick King-Smith and Jill Tomlinson

Background
These two opening sections introduce us to the stories in different ways. *The Hodgeheg* begins with dialogue that introduces the theme of the book – the dangers of roads for hedgehogs. When read in conjunction with the blurb from the previous text, it can be seen that the particular problem is crossing the road to the park. Roads are dangerous places for the children as well as for hedgehogs, so the context will be familiar. The opening of *The Otter Who Wanted to Know* uses description, rather than dialogue, and introduces the main character and the setting. The children are less likely to be familiar with the habitat and habits of sea otters, so this opening description provides a context for the story. The dialogue in the second half of the extract reveals more about the character of Pat, building on the information in the blurb.

The different content and approach of these two opening sections allows the children to consider different ways of beginning stories, which will help to develop their own writing.

Shared reading and discussing the text
● Introduce the texts and recap the information from the blurbs, re-reading if necessary. Ask the children what they expect to be in each opening and why the beginning of a story is important.
● Read the first extract with the children, modelling expression and intonation, reading strategies – reminding them particularly of the use of syllables for reading longer words – and noting compound words.
● What do we learn from this opening section? (Ensure that the children understand the colloquialism *copped it*.) Where was Auntie Betty going? What is the problem?
● Remind the children of the use of speech marks, highlighting the words actually spoken by the two characters. Give the children copies of the text and ask them to read the dialogue in pairs, taking the parts of Ma and Pa, using appropriate expression.

● Read the second extract. What do we learn? (If available, show the children a picture of a sea otter and tell them some facts.) Ask the children to tell each other about Pat – what do we learn about her character?
● Ask the children to discuss which of the two openings they think is most effective. Which makes them want to read on and why? Why did the two authors choose to begin their stories in different ways?
● Highlight *fur, her* and *first* in the second extract. Note the common *er* sound but different spellings (note also *third* in the first extract). Brainstorm more words containing the *er* phoneme, classifying the different spellings.

Activities
● Rewrite the first paragraph of the second text in the present tense. Ask the children to discuss the difference in meaning (introducing the idea of past/present at an appropriate level). Note that most stories are told in the past tense. Highlight the words that have changed (verbs) and ask the children to compare the past and present tenses. Note that some have *ed* endings, some have a different word. Ask the children to find other -*ed* verbs, and some might be able to spot irregular past tenses (for example, *kept*). Put some regular and irregular present tenses on the board and ask the children to discuss their past tense. Stop at some of the other common irregular words (from Appendix 1 of the National Literacy Strategy) and ask children to use whiteboards to practise spelling using Look–Say–Cover–Write–Check.
● The children can add to their notes on each story, showing how each extract introduces further information about settings, characters and themes.
● Give mixed-ability groups a selection of books at appropriate reading levels. Ask them to read the openings and note how the authors have chosen to begin – through dialogue or narrative. Ask them to consider for each whether they are 'drawn in' and want to read more.

2: 3: W1: to secure phonemic spellings from previous 5 terms

2: 3: W2: to reinforce work on discriminating syllables in reading and spelling from previous term

2: 3: W8: to spell common irregular words from Appendix List 1

2: 3: S1: to read text aloud with intonation and expression appropriate to the grammar and punctuation

indicates how dialogue was 'said'

colloquial

compound word

dialogue gets reader straight into the action – problem is introduced immediately but not main character or any scene setting/ description

Story openings

Extract 1

note punctuation for reading aloud

compound word

The Hodgeheg

"YOUR AUNTIE BETTY has copped it," said Pa Hedgehog to Ma.

"Oh, no!" cried Ma. "Where?"

"Just down the road. Opposite the newsagent's. Bad place to cross, that."

introduces problem – roads are dangerous for hedgehogs

"Everywhere's a bad place to cross nowadays," said Ma. "The traffic's dreadful. Do you realise, Pa, that's the third this year, and all on my side of the family too. First there was Grandfather, then my second cousin once removed, and now poor old Auntie Betty…"

big family! it is a personal problem

Extract 2

The Otter Who Wanted to Know

background information about sea otters

Pat was a young sea otter. She was rolling over and over in the sea, washing her fur. She gave it a final wash. Then she lay on her back, turned up her toes and the tip of her broad tail, and floated on the sea for a rest.

irregular past tense forms

same spelling ('oa') but different sound

regular past tense form

Bobby was a sea otter too. He had just noticed Pat for the first time. Although she was small she seemed to know how to look after herself. He went over to her.

"Hello," he said. "What are you doing?"

tells us about Pat – seems confident

Pat kept her eyes shut. "Nothing," she said. She knew better than to talk to strange otters.

Bobby paddled round beside her, and lay on the water too.

irregular past tense form 'said'; important for dialogue

"Good," he said, "I've got nothing to do either, so I'll do it with you."

persistent

"The sea's quite big," said Pat. "There's plenty of room for both of us."

dialogue

"Yes, it is big," Bobby said. But he wasn't going to be put off as easily as that. "It's called the Pacific, you know."

a bit arrogant, trying to get rid of him

"I didn't know that," Pat said, interested at once. "Why?"

scene setting

questions! interested now because Bobby can tell her things

2: 3: S3: to use standard forms of verbs in speaking and writing, e.g. *catch/caught, see/saw, go/went* and to use the past tense consistently for narration

2: 3: T1: to reinforce and apply their word-level skills through shared and guided reading

2: 3: T7: to compare books by different authors on similar themes; to evaluate, giving reasons

2: 3: T9: through shared and guided writing to apply phonological, graphic knowledge and sight vocabulary to spell words accurately

Scene setting
by Dick King-Smith and Jill Tomlinson

Background

These extracts develop key elements of the two stories, building particularly on ideas about the settings and themes. The extract from *The Hodgeheg* follows immediately on from the previous extract, and we discover why the Park is such a desirable destination, worth the risk of crossing the road. The extract from *The Otter Who Wanted to Know* comes from a little later in the book. Pat and Bobby have become friends, and Bobby, being older, is able to answer some of Pat's many questions about life. This section tells the reader more about the setting and introduces the key theme of the story – the problem of finding food (making a further link with *The Hodgeheg*).

The extracts offer opportunity for discussion on different ways of approaching scene setting. In the first, the scene is set through description; in the second, this is done through dialogue. The children will be able to consider the importance of the setting and how it influences events and behaviour, building on work done in Term 2.

Shared reading and discussing the text

● Remind the children of the previous extracts and ask them to retell what they have learned so far about the stories, drawing on their earlier work on the key story elements.
● Read the first extract and ask the children which elements this builds on – drawing out setting and problem. Note that the main character (introduced in the blurb) has not yet appeared in the story.
● Read extract 2 and ask what is learned, noting that the key problem in the story is introduced.
● Ask the children to compare the problems in each story, noting similarities and differences.
● Draw the children's attention to the fact that in each case the problem is directly related to the setting, by suggesting other settings and noting how this would affect the problem.
● Ask the children to discuss in pairs how they think the problem of each story might be resolved, drawing on the extracts read so far.

● Read the two extracts again and ask the children to note how each is written – considering the difference between description and dialogue. Why do they think Dick King-Smith gives such a detailed description of the Park and its attractions? Which extract is more effective at developing understanding of the settings and problems?
● Highlight *feasting, dwelt* and *slithered* from *The Hodgeheg* extract. Check understanding of the words and ask the children to think of other words that could be used instead, using a thesaurus if appropriate. (Remind them of Term 2 work on synonyms.) Consider the author's choices and whether they are effective. Can they find more powerful words?

Activities

● Ask the children to describe the Park to each other. Ask one child to share his/her description with the class and write this up, or record it on tape. Compare it with the original, noting differences. Pick out descriptive words and phrases that add detail and interest to the story.
● Ask the children to work in pairs and note two or three words or phrases to describe the setting of *The Otter Who Wanted to Know*, thinking about sight, sound, smell, taste and touch. Share and record ideas.
● Model one or two sentences to begin a description of the setting for *The Otter Who Wanted to Know*, drawing attention to the past tense and making occasional mistakes (using present tense or incorrect past tense forms).
● The children can now write their own descriptions, drawing on the shared ideas and the model. Use one child's description, in guided writing or a plenary, to consider how to improve it with the use of more effective words and phrases. Less able children could draw the setting and write words and phrases to describe it. More able children could use a thesaurus to find effective words for description.
● Ask the children to add again to their notes on the stories – recording additional information about settings, problems and characters.

2: 3: T3: to notice the difference between spoken and written forms through retelling known stories; compare oral versions with the written text

2: 3: T7: to compare books by different authors on similar themes; to evaluate, giving reasons

Scene setting

Extract 1

compare with the Dursleys' home in the Harry Potter stories to check children's understanding

setting conveyed through description

The Hodgeheg

They were sitting in a flower-bed at their home, the garden of Number 5A of a row of <u>semi-detached houses in a suburban street.</u> On the other side of the road was a Park, very popular with local hedgehogs on account of the (good) hunting it offered. As well as worms and slugs and snails, which they could find in their own gardens, there were special attractions in the Park. Mice lived under the (Bandstand,) feasting on the crumbs dropped from listeners' sandwiches; frogs (dwelt) in the Lily-Pond, and in the Ornamental Gardens grass-snakes (slithered) through the (shrubbery.) All these creatures were regarded as great (delicacies) by the hedgehogs, and they could never resist the occasional night's sport in the Park. But to reach it, they had to cross the busy road.

effective description makes reader understand how tempting it is – irresistible!

consider author's word choices; alternatives? which is most effective?

a covered platform where bands play

area planted with shrubs – large woody plants

lived

slid along

special things to eat

Extract 2

they are opening mussels and oysters in order to eat the edible part inside

shellfish: shells with edible flesh inside

The Otter Who Wanted to Know

"I can manage (mussels,) Pat said, "but I don't think I could open one of those (oysters)"

"There may not be any (oysters) left to open soon," said Bobby.

"Why shouldn't there be any left?" asked Pat.

"Because there are (so many of us,) said Bobby, "that it's getting harder and harder to find food."

"No one else seems to have found (this place,) Pat said. "Let's go and hunt for some more, and this time I'll see if I can break one myself."

They dived among the rocks. They looked and looked, and felt with their paws. Finally they each found one rock oyster. <u>They had to come up to the surface of the water to breathe again.</u>

the problem: too many otters, not enough oysters

setting conveyed through dialogue

there are so few oysters that it takes a lot of searching to find just one

setting through description

more background information about sea otters: they are mammals – they cannot breathe under water

2: 3: W10: to use synonyms and other alternative words/phrases that express same or similar meanings; to collect, discuss similarities and shades of meaning and use to extend and enhance writing

Characterisation

by Dick King-Smith and Jill Tomlinson

Extracts 1 and 2

Background

The last two extracts from the stories allow children to develop greater understanding of the two main characters. Max is introduced and his character is revealed through narrative and dialogue. He listens to his father's lecture about road safety, and determines to solve the problem of getting to the Park. Bobby has been showing Pat more delicacies, when he spots danger. The children will now be able to draw on what they have learned about the stories – settings, themes, characters – and the story-telling devices – description and dialogue – to write their own stories, based on one of them.

Shared reading and discussing the text

● Recap the previous extracts and what has been learned about the two stories in terms of settings, themes and characters.

● Read the extract from *The Hodgeheg*. Explain that in-between the two paragraphs, Pa gives a lecture about road safety. Ask the children what they learn about Max.

● Read the text from *The Otter Who Wanted to Know* and discuss the new information about Pat. What do the children think of her actions? How will she escape from the storm? (You might share the actual outcome with them.)

● Share words and phrases about the two characters and ask the children to justify their suggestions for these with reference to the text. Note that characterisation is built up through description and dialogue.

● Highlight *hastily, carefully, safely*. Point out that they describe *how* someone does something. Give examples of other words ending in *-ly*, for example *merrily, painfully, nicely*, and explore spelling patterns.

Activities

● The children can build up a character profile, using the words and phrases shared above to help them. Tell the children that they will use this information to write a story about Max or Pat. Ask them to decide which character they want to write about (individually or in pairs).

● Ask the children to discuss in pairs what might happen in their chosen story. Share some ideas and demonstrate how to plan a story.

● Ask the children to think about their story opening. Write two opening sentences for the story planned above, one a narrative and one a dialogue, highlighting the punctuation and re-reading to check for sense. Read again and ask the children which they prefer.

● The children can now begin to write their own stories, individually or in pairs. They should first plan the story, and share it with a partner (or another pair), explaining what will happen. Less able children may need help to structure their story plan. They could then use a storyboard to draw the story in six steps for example, writing a single sentence for each. Encourage more able children to use description and dialogue in their stories and to use speech marks to identify dialogue. They might also include *-ly* words to describe how actions are done, to add interest to their writing. They should then write their opening sentence, which can again be shared (perhaps with the whole class) and evaluated.

● As they continue, remind the children to draw on the notes they have already made about the shared texts. Encourage them to read their stories aloud as they write to check for sense and punctuation. Use guided writing to include an effective ending for their stories.

Extension/further reading

The children's stories can be made into books, for use as a reading resource in the classroom. If they are available, read the rest of both books to the children. Ask them to write a review; you might provide a word bank (*exciting, funny, unusual*) or a writing frame. Read other books by the same authors, for example any of the stories in Jill Tomlinson's series. Dick King-Smith has written many other animal stories with similar themes, including *King Max the Last* (sequel to *The Hodgeheg*, Puffin), *Sophie's Adventures* (Walker Books), *Harry's Mad, The Sheep-Pig* and *Blessu* (all Puffin).

2: 3: T10: to write sustained stories, using their knowledge of story elements: narrative, settings, characterisation, dialogue and the language of story

Characterisation

Extract 1

The Hodgeheg

Almost from the moment his eyes had opened, while his prickles were still soft and rubbery, Max had shown promise of being a bright boy; and by now his eyes, his ears, and his wits were all as sharp as his spines.

"What are you talking about, Ma?" he said.

"Nothing," said Ma hastily.

"You wouldn't be talking about nothing," said Max, "or there wouldn't be any point in talking."

Max listened carefully. Then he said, "Do humans cross the road?"

"I suppose so," said Pa.

"But don't they get killed?"

"Don't think so," said Pa. "Never seen one lying in the road. Which I would have if they did."

"Well then," said Max, "how do they get across safely?"

"You tell me, son. You tell me," said Pa.

" I will," said Max. "I will."

description tells reader about Max's character

she doesn't want to upset Max by talking about Auntie Betty

note spelling of adverbs ending in '-ly'

we also learn about Max from what he says and does

figurative language to describe Max

cheeky!

Pa gives lecture about road safety

clever boy; thinking hard

determined to work out problem

Extract 2

The Otter Who Wanted to Know

Bobby didn't reply. He was looking at the sky.

"I don't like the look of that," he said. "Those are storm clouds and the sea is getting choppy. We must get farther out to sea."

"Why?" asked Pat.

"Because the waves will smash us against the rocks!"

"I can't see any waves," said Pat. "I'm going back to that place we found yesterday. I fancy another rock oyster."

"No, you mustn't," said Bobby. "That's just where the waves will begin!"

But he was too late. Pat wasn't listening. She had gone round to the inlet and was under the water hunting for oysters. She found one. But when she came up with it she couldn't lie still to smash it, because the waves were breaking over the rocks. They nearly threw her onto a sharp edge.

Bobby older and more experienced

always asking questions

we learn about Pat's character through description and dialogue

rough

isn't prepared to accept Bobby's advice

taking a risk for a treat

gets into difficulty because she doesn't listen or heed advice

2: 3: T12: to write simple evaluations of books read and discussed giving reasons

2: 3: W7: to spell words with common suffixes, e.g. -*ful*, -*ly*

Little Red Riding Pig

by Dick King-Smith

Background

Dick King-Smith has taken a traditional tale, modernised the setting and language, and reversed the power-relations of grandmother and the wolf. The 'heroine' is now a pig (clearly one of the author's favourites, his most famous being Babe, the Sheep-Pig), who is small, rides a mountain bike, and is a ginger colour, hence her name. The children will have little difficulty predicting the outcome from this extract (the wolf obligingly looks into the fat pig's wide open mouth and…), and will enjoy the reversal of roles. The children will be able to compare this story with a traditional version (see page 42), and with other stories by Dick King-Smith, and begin to express preferences.

Shared reading and discussing the text

● Read and discuss the title. What does the title mean? What is this story about? Remind the children of the original tale (refer to the extracts in Term 2, page 42), and discuss the name. Ask the children to speculate about this name. You might give the character's description (above).

● Ask the children to tell the traditional tale to each other in pairs. Listen and note where the children use language from the original. Set the scene for this extract – Red Riding Pig is going to visit her grandmother.

● Read the extract, using appropriate 'voices' in the dialogue (and for the wolf's thoughts). What do the children think is going to happen? Encourage predictions, drawing on the original story and this extract. Ask them for personal responses, expressing views and justifying them with reference to the text.

● Ask the children to discuss the story and compare it with the traditional version. Ask them to think about setting, characters, events and language. Draw out the similarities and differences, noting particularly the role of the grandmother and that of the wolf. Notice that grandmother seems to be in control of the situation! Where is Little Red Riding Pig? Who is going to be eaten? How does the story end?

● Read some of the dialogue again, asking the children to consider the language used, particularly by the wolf. What does this tell us about him? Consider the effect on the reader of the humorous language (echoes of American gangster movies perhaps).

● Remind the children of the use of speech marks to identify the words spoken by characters. Note the phrases (*said the wolf…*) that tell the reader who is speaking. Give the children copies of the text and ask them to highlight these phrases. Point out the repetition of *said*, and the alternatives in places (*replied, asked, called*). Brainstorm other ways of saying things, for example *whispered, shouted, cried, exclaimed* – demonstrating if necessary.

Activities

● The children can write endings for the story, drawing on predictions made earlier about the fate of the wolf and grandmother, and the arrival of Little Red Riding Pig. Less able children can narrate their story endings onto tape or to a scribe. More able children could include dialogue in their writing, drawing on the language of the text, and using speech marks.

● The children can collect examples from their reading of other words for introducing dialogue, and make collections for future use in writing. They could also read prepared sentences in different ways in response to cards prompting them to *whisper, yell, whine…*

● Ask groups of children to role-play the story, drawing on appropriate language for dialogue.

Extension/further reading

The children could write alternative versions of other familiar tales. Read alternative versions by Dick King-Smith, for example 'The Owl and the Pussycat (the Sequel)', 'Goldipig and the Three Bears', 'The Ugly Duckling', 'Hogsel and Gruntel', 'The Princess and the Pig' – all in *More Animal Stories* by Dick King-Smith (Penguin). Compare with other stories by the same author (including *The Hodgeheg*) that are not drawn from traditional tales. Which do the children prefer and why?

2: 3: T3: to notice the difference between spoken and written forms through re-telling known stories; compare oral versions with the written text

2: 3: T4: to compare books by same author: settings, characters, themes; to evaluate and form preferences, giving reasons

beginning of familiar title

she rides a mountain bike

very casual, colloquial language; possibly American gangster movie language

missing 'g' suggests accent of wolf

reader is told wolf's thoughts but left to infer Lttle Red Riding Pig's and her grandmother's

rather innocent and naïve

Grandmother seems calm and in control; she flatters him

it is almost as if she knows how the story goes

an open space in the forest

~ = note repetitious 'said'

alternatives to 'said'

baby pig

figurative

Red Riding Hood's line in the original tale

why? so she couldn't see his teeth?

familiar lines but different speaker and context

showing his teeth

Little Red Riding Pig

Cycling through a forest glade she met a wolf.

"Hold it right there, baby," said the wolf.

Little Red Riding Pig held it.

"Where you headin'?" said the wolf.

"To visit my grandmother," replied Little Red Riding Pig.

The wolf thought quickly. Not a lot of meat on this piglet, he said to himself, but the granny – now she might make a square meal.

"Your granny kinda fat?" he asked in a casual way.

"Oh yes!" said Little Red Riding Pig. "She's very fat."

"Sure like to meet her," said the wolf. "She live around here some place?"

"Oh yes!" said Little Red Riding Pig, and she told the wolf how to get to her grandmother's house, and away he went.

When he arrived, he knocked on the door and a voice called, "Come in, my dear," so he did.

There, lying in bed, was the fattest pig the wolf had ever seen.

"Goodness me!" said the pig. "I thought you were my little granddaughter."

"'Fraid not ma'am," said the wolf.

"But I see now," said Little Red Riding Pig's grandmother, "that you are in fact a handsome stranger. What big ears you have!"

All the better to hear you with, thought the wolf, but he kept his mouth shut.

"And what big eyes you have!"

All the better to see you with, thought the wolf, but he said nothing, merely opening his jaws in a kind of silent laugh.

"And what big teeth you have!" said the fat pig, and before the wolf could think about that, she went on, "Which reminds me, I have the toothache. I should be so grateful if you could look and see which tooth is causing the trouble."

2: 3: T6: to read, respond imaginatively, recommend and collect examples of humorous stories, extracts, poems

2: 3: W10: to use synonyms and other alternative words/phrases that express same or similar meanings; to collect, discuss similarities and shades of meaning and use to extend and enhance writing

The Really Ugly Duckling

by Jon Scieszka

Background

This is a new take on a classic fairy tale by Hans Christian Andersen. This subverted retelling works on the assumption that the reader knows the original and knows to expect the traditional happy ending. (This is reinforced by the ugly duckling's own belief that it will turn into a swan.) The surprise and humour lie in the unexpected twist, and children will enjoy the anarchic feel of overturning 'happy ever after'.

Shared reading and discussing the text

● Tell the children that they are going to read a traditional tale and ask what they remember about such stories.

● Show the children the title and ask if anyone knows the story and could tell it to the class. If no one knows it, tell a brief version yourself.

● Read the story, keeping the enlarged sentences concealed. Note the traditional opening and pause before the last part. What might happen? Read the ending. Ask the children to comment – were they surprised? Why? Did they enjoy the story? Why/why not? Consider how this differs from the original and from other traditional tales.

● Focus on *The really ugly duckling heard these people… better than anything in the pond.* Why wasn't the duckling worried about being ugly? It is almost as if he has read the story about himself!

● Read the text again together and consider the language of the story, particularly phrases such as *regular-looking, nice-looking bunch* and *Boy, he's really ugly.* Ask the children if phrases like this are usually found in traditional stories. Some of the children might recognise them as more likely to be found in films (spoken language), particularly American. Note how they develop the humour of the text. Ask the children to change them into more familiar traditional story language.

● Highlight *really* in the text. Ask the children what it means, noting that it adds strength to *ugly* and also means 'truly.' Look for the shorter word within it, underlining *real*. Note the *-ly* ending (suffix). Repeat for *probably,* noting the spelling change from *probable.* (Note *ugly* also has *-ly,* although not a suffix because it hasn't been added to another word.) Ask the children to suggest other words with the suffix *–ly,* noting where spelling changes occur.

Activities

● Brainstorm other traditional tales on the board. Choose one or two and consider ideas to subvert them. In shared writing, make a plan to subvert one story (such as Cinderella where the fairy godmother does not arrive). Model the traditional opening of the story, incorporating some of the language of *The Really Ugly Duckling* (for example, *'Boy, were those sisters ugly'*). Discuss how the story will end in this new version.

● The children can now choose a story and write their own subversion, planning the storyline (perhaps in pairs) first. Encourage the children to read their stories aloud as they write to check for sense and punctuation. Less able children may need to work with support, to plan a group story. Alternatively, they can be given a story starter. Encourage more able children to incorporate the colloquial language of the *Really Ugly Duckling* extract.

● The children can read their stories aloud with appropriate expression to ensure the surprise element. Ask others to evaluate for effect, humour, surprise and language.

Extension/further reading

Collect the children's stories for presentation in a class book, perhaps alongside copies of the original stories. Record the children's stories onto tape to be used as a reading and listening resource. Read a more traditional version of the original story such as *The Ugly Duckling* by Ian Beck (Orchard). Jon Scieszka has subverted other traditional tales in *The Stinky Cheese Man* (Puffin). Babette Cole has also subverted traditional tales in *Prince Cinders* and *Princess Smartypants* (Puffin). See also Roald Dahl's *Revolting Rhymes* (Puffin).

2: 3: T6: to read, respond imaginatively, recommend and collect examples of humorous stories, extracts, poems

2: 3: T11: to use humorous [stories] as a structure for children to write their own by adaptation, mimicry or substitution; to invent own riddles, language puzzles, jokes, nonsense sentences etc., derived from reading; write tongue-twisters or alliterative sentences; select words with care, re-reading and listening to their effect

not in original

traditional story opening

traditional scene setting

allusion to the traditional happy ending

surprise twist – no traditional fairy tale happy ending; an ordinary everyday ending – the real world!

typographical features add to surprise and emphasis

colloquial language, not typical of traditional tales

suffix '-ly'

American dialect

sounds like he knows what happens in traditional version himself

The Really Ugly Duckling

Once upon a time there was a mother duck and a father duck who had seven baby ducklings. Six of them were regular-looking ducklings. The seventh was a really ugly duckling.
Everyone used to say, "What a nice-looking bunch of ducklings—all except that one. Boy, he's really ugly." The really ugly duckling heard these people, but he didn't care. He knew that one day he would probably grow up to be a swan and be bigger and look better than anything in the pond.

Well, as it turned out, he was just a really ugly duckling. And he grew up to be just a really ugly duck. The End.

2: 3: S1: to read text aloud with intonation and expression appropriate to the grammar and punctuation

2: 3: W7: to spell words with common suffixes, e.g. -ful, -ly

A Big Bare Bear by Robert Heidbreder

Background

Robert Heidbreder's poetry for children is often based on patterns of rhythm and sound. This is a humorous verse, which plays with repeated rhymes and particularly with the homophones *bare* and *bear*. The children will enjoy listening to and reciting the repetitions and the sounds, and the rather naughty ending appeals to the child's sense of humour. The poem offers the opportunity to explore spelling patterns in words, focusing on the *air* phoneme and its varied written forms. This can lead to investigation of words with similar spelling patterns but different sounds.

Shared reading and discussing the text

● Read the title and discuss the homophones, using dictionaries if necessary to distinguish between the two words.

● Read the rhyme with the children, ensuring that attention is paid to the punctuation to make sense. You might cover up the last two words initially to highlight and savour them – words not often used in the classroom!

● Ask the children to retell the 'story', discussing the characters and events.

● Ask the children for responses. Was it funny? Why? Did they enjoy it? Why? Encourage them to refer directly to the poem to justify views.

● Read the poem again to enjoy the sounds and rhythms, encouraging all the children to join in with the rhyming words at least.

● Give the children copies of the poem and ask them to highlight all the rhyming words. Collect these on the board and look at spellings. Revise spellings of the *ie* phoneme (*high*/*sky*). Note the silent *b* on *thumb* (introduce other such words if appropriate, for example *lamb, climb*).

● Focus on words containing the *air* phoneme (*bare*, *bear*, *hairy*), reminding the children of the different spellings. Brainstorm other words with the same phoneme and categorise them according to spelling (including *there*, *where* if appropriate).

● Put *bear* and *dear* on the board and ask the children to read them. Ensure that all the children are clear that the words have the same spelling pattern but different sounds. Brainstorm other words with the *ear* phoneme and note that there are different ways of spelling this as well. Draw attention to the homophones *dear*/*deer*.

Activities

● Tell the children that they are going to make up simple poems using the rhymes discussed above. Model the first line, for example *The bare bear combed his hair*. Ask the children to choose another rhyming word and write another sentence, this time beginning with *The hairy bear…* Set it out under the first, noting that this makes it look like a poem. Ask pairs to compose the next two lines.

● The children can write their own poems, beginning with the shared model. Less able children can work in a group with support to compose poems. Alternatively, use a writing frame with the sentence starter and a rhyming word, or the whole sentence except the rhyme. More able children could write similar poems beginning with *The dear deer…*

● Give the children words containing the *ear* phoneme and ask them to categorise them by spelling. Use these for spelling and handwriting practice.

● Give the children copies of the poem with the rhyming words omitted to complete, choosing the correct spellings.

● The children can prepare the poem for performance, in pairs or groups. Encourage reading with expression and taking account of punctuation, noting where there are commas and full stops and where the reading should flow.

Extension/further reading

The children can copy out the poem for display or for collection in a class anthology, explaining the language play and saying why they liked it. Some children might enjoy competing to write the longest sentence using as many of the rhyming words as possible (*air* and/or *ear*).

2: 3: W1: to secure phonemic spellings from previous 5 terms

2: 3: W3: discriminate, spell and read the phonemes *ear* (hear) and *ea* (head)

2: 3: W6: to investigate words which have the same spelling patterns but different sounds

homophones: same sound, different spelling

take account of punctuation for reading, commas and full stops

different spellings of 'air' phoneme

A Big Bare Bear

A big bare bear
  bought a bear balloon, ᴿ
For a big bear trip
  to the bare, bare moon. ᴿ
A hairy bear
  saw the bare bear fly
On the big bear trip
  in the bare, bare sky.
The hairy bear
  took a jet up high
To catch the bear
  in the big bare sky.
The hairy bear
  flew his jet right by
The bear balloon
  in the big bare sky.
He popped the balloon
  with his hairy thumb,
And the bare bear fell
  on his big bum bum.

Robert Heidbreder

rhymes

different spellings of 'ie' phoneme

silent 'b'

fun, slightly rude!

2: 3: T6: to read, respond imaginatively, recommend and collect examples of humorous stories, extracts, poems

2: 3: T8: to discuss meanings of words and phrases that create humour, and sound effects in poetry, e.g. nonsense poems, tongue-twisters, riddles, and to classify poems into simple types; to make class anthologies

On the Ning Nang Nong

by Spike Milligan

Background

Spike Milligan is well known for his nonsense verse. He loved to play with words and sounds, experimenting in much the same way that young children do. One of Milligan's strongest poetic influences was Edward Lear, the 'inventor' of the limerick (see page 96). Nonsense appeals to most children and is perhaps particularly valuable for reluctant readers. This poem uses onomatopoeic sounds to create musical verse, which is clearly meant to be read aloud and performed.

Shared reading and discussing the text

● Read the poem through to allow the children to enjoy the sounds, re-reading if appropriate with the children joining in.

● Ask for observations. Did they enjoy it? Why? What makes it funny? What is it about?

● Discuss the poet, telling the children that Spike Milligan enjoyed writing nonsense verse, and experimenting with words and sounds. Ask them to picture the imaginary place.

● Give the children copies of the poem and ask them to highlight the rhyming words. Give them time in pairs to repeat the words, enjoying the onomatopoeic effect. Ask them to describe what the words sound like. The children can experiment with other words with similar sounds (*ding dang dong, sing sang song, bish bash bosh*). Note the alliteration and that only the vowel changes.

● Ask the children why there are exclamation marks at the end of most of the lines, noting that they show how the words should be read to emphasise the sounds.

● Look at the structure of the poem, describing the rhyming pattern of lines, and the repeated phrases in the second part. Ask an adult to read the poem to less able children and get them to identify syllables by clapping.

Activities

● Put up a doctored version of the text with the 'sound' words and the nouns omitted. Tell the children that you are going to write a new poem by substituting different words. Remind them of the onomatopoeic strings they suggested above and ask them to discuss and suggest other possibilities for the animals (and trees and teapots!), ensuring that the same number of syllables is used. Write a new first line by selecting one of the onomatopoeic strings, reminding the children that it is the vowel that changes. Count the syllables with the children to ensure that the rhythm is maintained. Rewrite the second line, choosing a single-syllable animal to replace *cows*, and a new rhyming word at the end. Read both lines to check for rhythm and sound. Repeat for the third line, noting that this time two syllables are needed to replace *monkeys*.

● Give the children their own copies of the poem with words missing and they should now be able to continue the poem from the model (or begin their own). Remind them about maintaining the rhythm by reading aloud and counting syllables during composition. Less able children can work with support to compose a group poem. They might just work with sounds, orally, creating rhyming strings, to develop phonological awareness.

● In guided writing, consider the penultimate line, which depends on the rhyme selected.

● Ask the children to experiment with other onomatopoeic words and present them to illustrate the sounds they make (showing *splash!*, for example, falling into water).

Extension/further reading

Set the poems (the original and/or the children's compositions) to music, using tuned and untuned percussion instruments to accompany the rhythms and sounds. Read other Spike Milligan poetry and ask the children to choose and justify favourites for inclusion in a class anthology of nonsense verse. See, for example, *A Children's Treasury of Milligan* (Virgin Books) – a collection of some of his earlier volumes. See also Michael Rosen's *Book of Very Silly Poems* (Puffin) and Edward Lear's *Gromboolian Poems* (Macmillan) for other nonsense poems.

2: 3: W2: to reinforce work on discriminating syllables in reading and spelling from previous term

2: 3: T1: to reinforce and apply their word-level skills through shared and guided reading

2: 3: T6: to read, respond imaginatively, recommend and collect examples of humorous stories, extracts, poems

only the vowels change

alliteration

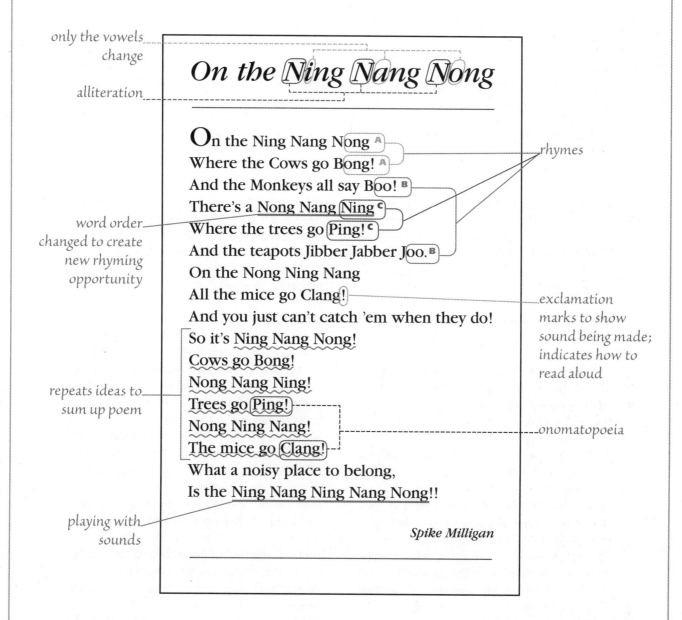

On the Ning Nang Nong

On the Ning Nang Nong ᴬ
Where the Cows go Bong! ᴬ
And the Monkeys all say Boo! ᴮ
There's a Nong Nang Ning ᶜ
Where the trees go Ping! ᶜ
And the teapots Jibber Jabber Joo. ᴮ
On the Nong Ning Nang
All the mice go Clang!
And you just can't catch 'em when they do!
So it's Ning Nang Nong!
Cows go Bong!
Nong Nang Ning!
Trees go Ping!
Nong Ning Nang!
The mice go Clang!
What a noisy place to belong,
Is the Ning Nang Ning Nang Nong!!

Spike Milligan

word order changed to create new rhyming opportunity

repeats ideas to sum up poem

playing with sounds

rhymes

exclamation marks to show sound being made; indicates how to read aloud

onomatopoeia

2: 3: T8: to discuss meanings of words and phrases that create humour, and sound effects in poetry, e.g. nonsense poems, tongue-twisters, riddles, and to classify poems into simple types; to make class anthologies

2: 3: T11: to use humorous verse as a structure for children to write their own by adaptation, mimicry or substitution; to invent own riddles, language puzzles, jokes, nonsense sentences etc., derived from reading; write tongue-twisters or alliterative sentences; select words with care, re-reading and listening to their effect

Sneezles

by AA Milne

Background

Two AA Milne poems were covered in Term 2 (see page 56), and introduced the children to the simple, childlike language and familiar topics of his poetry. 'Sneezles' describes Christopher Robin's day in bed with a cold. The children will recognise that the fuss this generates seems unnecessary for a mere cold (although in the early 20th century, even minor illness could be serious since there were fewer treatments). It is made clear at the end, however, that Christopher Robin finds the attention highly entertaining! The humour of the poem comes from the language play, using repetition of nonsense words to describe the symptoms of the cold.

Shared reading and discussing the text

● Remind the children of earlier poems by AA Milne.
● Read the title. What does it mean? Is it a real word? What word does it remind them of?
● Read the poem straight through to give a feel for the sounds and language, then re-read, stopping every now and then to check for understanding. Demonstrate strategies for reading unfamiliar words, focusing on word-level knowledge to help with rhymes.
● Ask the children for responses. Did they enjoy the poem and why? Did they find it funny? Do they get bundled into bed and have several doctors call when they have a cold? What does the last part of the poem tell us? Tell the children that colds were potentially more serious when this poem was written.
● Note the very short lines (like 'Happiness', see page 56) and demonstrate how to give the poem sense by using the punctuation.
● Ask the children to pick out the nonsense words and write them on the board. Give the children time to repeat the words to each other, enjoying the sounds and adding their own. Are any of them real words? (Only *measles*.) Consider how the poet has created the nonsense words, looking for the pattern in them. Why does the poet use these words?

Consider the effect of using the words as they should be written. (The addition of *-le* perhaps reflects the voice of the child and heightens the effect of the rhythms and rhymes.)
● Ask the children to highlight all the rhymes in the poem (perhaps taking sections in groups). Note different spellings for same sounds, revising long-vowel phonemes. Also note digraphs such as *ch* and *ph* (*<u>Ch</u>risto<u>ph</u>er*, *<u>ph</u>ysician*, *<u>ph</u>theezle*).
● Focus on the vowel phoneme in *bed* and *head*. Ask the children to suggest other words that use the *ea* spelling for this phoneme, beginning with rhyming words (*bread, dead*…), then others (*deaf, threat*…). Focus also on *said* (a useful exception).

Activities

● The children can prepare a dramatised reading of the poem, with small groups taking a section each. Use guided sessions to encourage reading with expression, using the punctuation to make sense of the lines. More able children might learn sections by heart.
● Ask the children to generate rhyming strings for *sneezle*, by changing the initial phoneme or blend. Encourage them to say the words aloud and enjoy the sounds they have made. They can then decide which might come from a real word and which are purely nonsense.
● The children can investigate spelling of the short *e* phoneme, generating a list (using dictionaries if appropriate) of those that use the *ea* spelling. Give them a wordsearch of *ea* words to find and practise spelling. Some children might explore the spelling of the *z* phoneme in the nonsense words, noting where the poem retains the original spelling and where it changes.

Extension/further reading

Read other AA Milne poems (see further reading, page 56). Poems in particular that play with words and sounds include 'The More It Snows' (in *The Hums of Pooh*) and 'The Three Foxes' (in *When We Were Very Young*).

2: 3: W1: to secure phonemic spellings from previous 5 terms

2: 3: W3: discriminate, spell and read the phonemes *ear* (hear) and *ea* (head)

2: 3: S1: to read text aloud with intonation and expression appropriate to the grammar and punctuation

2: 3: T1: to reinforce and apply their word-level skills through shared and guided reading

rhymes with 'bed' and 'head', a spelling exception which needs to be learned

revise 'ch' and 'ph' digraphs from Term 2

rhyme but different spellings

rhyme but different spellings

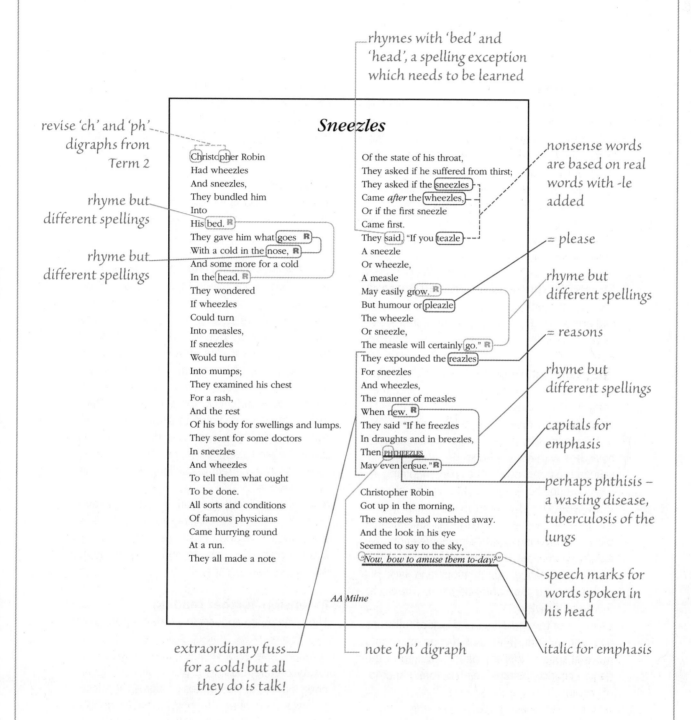

Sneezles

Christopher Robin
Had wheezles
And sneezles,
They bundled him
Into
His bed.
They gave him what goes
With a cold in the nose,
And some more for a cold
In the head.
They wondered
If wheezles
Could turn
Into measles,
If sneezles
Would turn
Into mumps;
They examined his chest
For a rash,
And the rest
Of his body for swellings and lumps.
They sent for some doctors
In sneezles
And wheezles
To tell them what ought
To be done.
All sorts and conditions
Of famous physicians
Came hurrying round
At a run.
They all made a note

Of the state of his throat,
They asked if he suffered from thirst;
They asked if the sneezles
Came *after* the wheezles,
Or if the first sneeze
Came first.
They said, "If you teazle
A sneeze
Or wheezle,
A measle
May easily grow.
But humour or pleazle
The wheeze
Or sneeze,
The measle will certainly go."
They expounded the reazles
For sneezles
And wheezles,
The manner of measles
When new.
They said "If he freezles
In draughts and in breezles,
Then PHTHEEZLES
May even ensue."

Christopher Robin
Got up in the morning,
The sneezles had vanished away.
And the look in his eye
Seemed to say to the sky,
"Now, how to amuse them to-day?"

AA Milne

nonsense words are based on real words with -le added

= please

rhyme but different spellings

= reasons

rhyme but different spellings

capitals for emphasis

perhaps phthisis – a wasting disease, tuberculosis of the lungs

speech marks for words spoken in his head

italic for emphasis

extraordinary fuss for a cold! but all they do is talk!

note 'ph' digraph

2: 3: T6: to read, respond imaginatively, recommend and collect examples of humorous stories, extracts, poems

2: 3: T8: to discuss meanings of words and phrases that create humour, and sound effects in poetry, e.g. nonsense poems, tongue-twisters, riddles, and to classify poems into simple types; to make class anthologies

Busy Day

by Michael Rosen

Background

This is another of Michael Rosen's poems (like 'Conversation' from Term 2, see page 64) that explores a familiar situation combining humorous wordplay with child-friendly, everyday language. It is a poem that needs to read aloud at speed to appreciate the ideas and sounds. The children will enjoy reading the poem aloud and the transparent structure will allow them to write their own poems in a similar style.

Shared reading and discussing the text

● Cover the title and read the poem, with gathering speed, pausing for breath only in the gaps, becoming breathless by the end! If possible, organise for another adult to read the second speaker's words.

● Ask the children for impressions. Did they enjoy it? Why? Was it funny? What is it about?

● Discuss what the title might be, then reveal it. Is it a good title? Why? Share experiences of busy days with no time to stop.

● Read the poem again, the children joining in, emphasising the sound of *pop*. Note how the short, sharp word reinforces the speed of the action. Discuss the onomatopoeic qualities of the word, drawing out its various meanings.

● Ask the children to discuss the layout of the poem, considering punctuation (and lack of) and gaps, and the contribution this makes to the poem's rhythm.

● Draw out the short lines and lack of full stops or commas, indicating that the poem should move at speed. Note the pause required at the gaps, a chance to draw breath before 'popping' off again.

● Note that the last 'verse' is a repetition of the first section, suggesting never-ending hurry (and reinforced by the ellipsis at the end).

● Focus on the question marks (the only punctuation), reminding the children of their use. Highlight *pop where? pop what?* Brainstorm other question words, noting that they commonly begin with *wh*.

● Read lines 8 and 9 aloud, noting that they are the same, and emphasising the difference in reading where there is a question mark. Note that questions do not always have a question word.

Activities

● Brainstorm other words that might suggest a busy day, such as *dash, zip* and *zoom*, and where you might be going in a hurry. Write a verse for a new poem, demonstrating how to keep the lines short to emphasise the speed.

● The children can write their own 'busy day' poems, using the ideas shared or their own. Encourage more able children to incorporate rhymes into their poems, for example *here/there, pool/school, down/town*. (Give less able children a copy of the poem with *pop* omitted and ask them to substitute another word.) Tell the children to check for sense and effect (pace) by reading aloud to a partner during composition. When completed, the poems should be read aloud to the class and evaluated, focusing on the effect of the language and the 'performance'.

● Ask the children to work in pairs to read 'Busy Day' aloud, developing fluency and pace with practice, taking turns to read each part.

● Let the children explore and illustrate other words that suggest speed.

Extension/further reading

The same poem appears in a different format in *Pilly Soems* (A&C Black). Ask the children to compare the two versions and express and justify preferences. Read other Michael Rosen poems that use the sounds of words for effect, for example 'Jibber jabber', 'Hobble gobble wobble', 'Tiffy taffy toffee' (also in *Pilly Soems*). Choose favourites to collect in a class anthology. Other poems where humour lies in the sounds of words include 'The Kettle' by Gwynneth Thurburn, 'Clocks and Watches', 'Higglety Pigglety Pop' and 'Summer Days' by Anne English (*The Puffin Book of Fantastic First Poems*).

2: 3: T6: to read, respond imaginatively, recommend and collect examples of humorous stories, extracts, poems

2: 3: T8: to discuss meanings of words and phrases that create humour, and sound effects in poetry, e.g. nonsense poems, tongue-twisters, riddles, and to classify poems into simple types; to make class anthologies

opposites emphasise the busyness

not a regular rhyme pattern, but rhyme is used occasionally

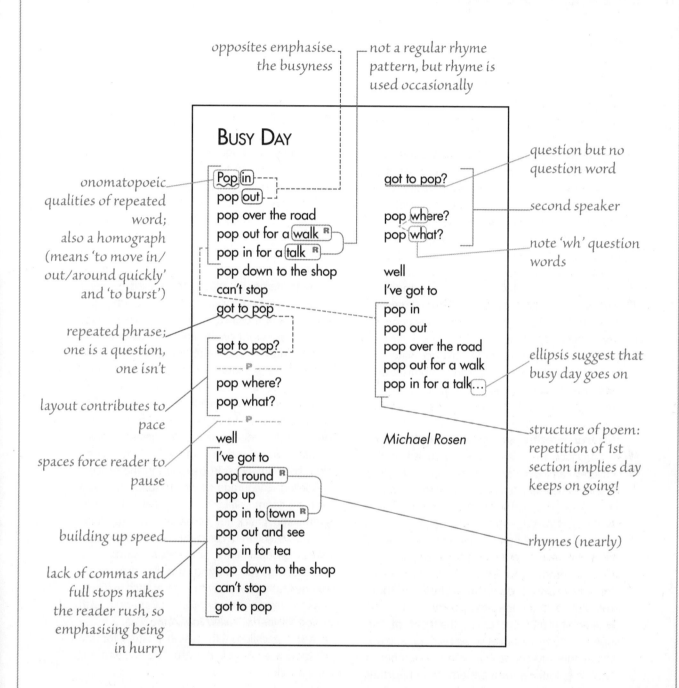

question but no question word

onomatopoeic qualities of repeated word; also a homograph (means 'to move in/ out/around quickly' and 'to burst')

second speaker

note 'wh' question words

repeated phrase; one is a question, one isn't

ellipsis suggest that busy day goes on

layout contributes to pace

spaces force reader to pause

structure of poem: repetition of 1st section implies day keeps on going!

building up speed

rhymes (nearly)

lack of commas and full stops makes the reader rush, so emphasising being in hurry

BUSY DAY

Pop in
pop out
pop over the road
pop out for a walk
pop in for a talk
pop down to the shop
can't stop
got to pop

got to pop?

pop where?
pop what?

well
I've got to
pop round
pop up
pop in to town
pop out and see
pop in for tea
pop down to the shop
can't stop
got to pop

got to pop?

pop where?
pop what?

well
I've got to
pop in
pop out
pop over the road
pop out for a walk
pop in for a talk...

Michael Rosen

2: 3: T11: to use humorous verse as a structure for children to write their own by adaptation, mimicry or substitution; to invent own riddles, language puzzles, jokes, nonsense sentences etc., derived from reading; write tongue-twisters or alliterative sentences; select words with care, re-reading and listening to their effect

2: 3: S1: to read text aloud with intonation and expression appropriate to the grammar and punctuation

Limericks

by Edward Lear, John Kitching,
Jack Ousbey and anon

Poems 1 to 5

Background

Edward Lear (1812–1888) remains the most famous writer of limericks, though the form was used as early as the beginning of the 18th century. Lear himself preferred the description 'nonsense poem'. Limericks are single-verse poems, with a very structured form – five lines, rhyming pattern AABBA, and, originally, 8–8–5–5–8 syllables in each line (although this is not always strictly adhered to). The form has been copied and adapted by many other poets (including Spike Milligan, a great admirer of Lear's comic poetry, see page 90). The limericks here include one by Lear and a selection of modern ones.

Children should be encouraged to recite and learn limericks to enjoy the nonsense and appreciate the rhythms. They will enjoy writing their own verses in the same tight structure.

Shared reading and discussing the text

● Introduce the term *limerick* and ask if the children are familiar with it. Read the first poem, which may remind them of the form.
● Ask for comments. Did they enjoy it, find it funny, and why?
● Read the verse again, asking the children to close their eyes and imagine the scene. Remind them of other nonsense verse they have read. Introduce Edward Lear – the children may know some of his other nonsense poetry.
● Read again, emphasising the beat of the poem. Clap the syllables while reading, and ask the children to count and note the number in each line, looking for a pattern. It is important that the children hear the 'tune' as well as count syllables, so read once more, beating the rhythm, then try 'sounding out' the poem using rhythms only ('de <u>da</u> da de <u>da</u> da de <u>da</u>').
● Ask the children to highlight the rhymes in the poem and explain the pattern.
● Read the second limerick. Again, ask the children to picture it and then analyse it as for the first limerick, noting the similar structure, drawing particular attention to the 'tune'.
● Read the remaining limericks, enjoying the 'pictures' and the language patterns. Compare rhymes and rhythms, noting the similarities. Note that they are all about a person with a 'peculiarity' (or a peculiar pet!).
● Explain *anon* to the children, drawing a link with traditional stories, passed by word of mouth, where the original teller is not known.

Activities

● Display a framework for a limerick, alongside a list of features. Write a starting line, using a familiar name or place, for example. Read aloud, counting syllables and checking the rhythm. Ask the children to brainstorm rhymes for the last word of the line. Choose one and 'think aloud' as you write the second line. Use the children's suggestions to write the third line, noting its different pattern. Brainstorm rhymes again, and model the fourth line. Now ask the children to work in pairs to write the last line, drawing on rhymes suggested earlier.
● The children can now have a go at writing their own limericks, in pairs, using the process modelled. Encourage them to experiment with sounds, count syllables and read aloud as they write, and check for sense and for rhythms. Less able children can work with support to write a group limerick. Some children may need suggestions for starting the limerick, using words that will be easy to rhyme, such as *There was a… from the moon/Mars/my street; …with a dog/cat/pet; …called Joe, Anne, Pat.*
● Ask the children to design posters for the classroom, explaining the structure and patterns of limericks.

Extension/further reading

The children can read and illustrate other limericks, expressing and justifying preferences. Read more Lear nonsense poems to the children and compare them with other poets read previously, such as Spike Milligan, AA Milne and Michael Rosen. See *A Book of Nonsense* by Edward Lear (Bodley Head), *The Complete Nonsense of Edward Lear* (Faber) and *Edward Lear's Gromboolian Poems* (Macmillan).

2: 3: T6: to read, respond imaginatively, recommend and collect examples of humorous stories, extracts, poems

2: 3: T8: to discuss meanings of words and phrases that create humour, and sound effects in poetry, e.g. nonsense poems, tongue-twisters, riddles, and to classify poems into simple types; to make class anthologies

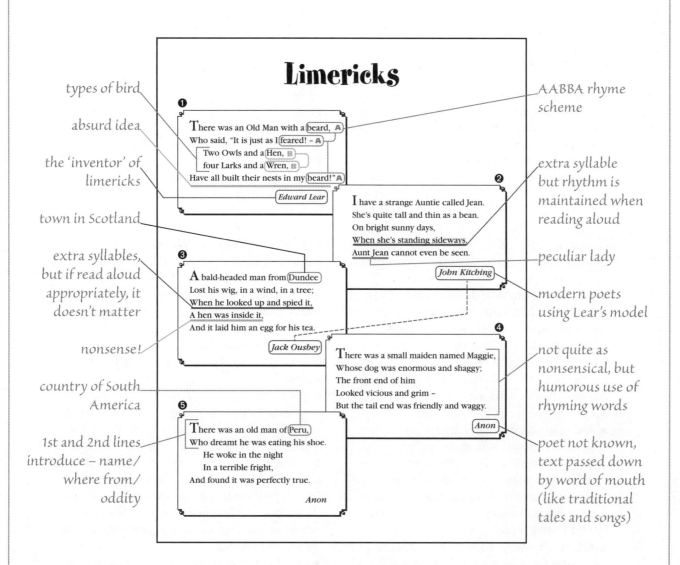

Limericks

types of bird

absurd idea

the 'inventor' of limericks

town in Scotland

extra syllables, but if read aloud appropriately, it doesn't matter

nonsense!

country of South America

1st and 2nd lines introduce – name/ where from/ oddity

❶

There was an Old Man with a beard, **A**
Who said, "It is just as I feared! – **A**
Two Owls and a Hen, **B**
four Larks and a Wren, **B**
Have all built their nests in my beard!" **A**

Edward Lear

❷

I have a strange Auntie called Jean.
She's quite tall and thin as a bean.
On bright sunny days,
When she's standing sideways,
Aunt Jean cannot even be seen.

John Kitching

❸

A bald-headed man from Dundee
Lost his wig, in a wind, in a tree;
When he looked up and spied it,
A hen was inside it,
And it laid him an egg for his tea.

Jack Ousbey

❹

There was a small maiden named Maggie,
Whose dog was enormous and shaggy;
The front end of him
Looked vicious and grim –
But the tail end was friendly and waggy.

Anon

❺

There was an old man of Peru,
Who dreamt he was eating his shoe.
He woke in the night
In a terrible fright,
And found it was perfectly true.

Anon

AABBA rhyme scheme

extra syllable but rhythm is maintained when reading aloud

peculiar lady

modern poets using Lear's model

not quite as nonsensical, but humorous use of rhyming words

poet not known, text passed down by word of mouth (like traditional tales and songs)

2: 3: T11: to use humorous verse as a structure for children to write their own by adaptation, mimicry or substitution; to invent own riddles, language puzzles, jokes, nonsense sentences etc., derived from reading; write tongue-twisters or alliterative sentences; select words with care, re-reading and listening to their effect

2: 3: S1: to read text aloud with intonation and expression appropriate to the grammar and punctuation

2: 3: W2: to reinforce work on discriminating syllables in reading and spelling from previous term

Teaser

by Tony Mitton

Background

Tony Mitton has written much poetry for children that plays with the sounds and meanings of words. Riddles are puzzles to be solved, often through a series of clues. This is a riddle in the form of a poem, which plays with the word 'elephants', using the word within the word. The humour lies in the unlikely opposition of *elephant* and *ant*, creating absurd images of monstrous ants. The extra dimension of rhyme in this riddle allows it to be read aloud with expression. The children will enjoy creating similar riddles, based on words within words.

Shared reading and discussing the text

● Read the poem with the children (without revealing the answer). Note the title, reflected at the end, asking the children to consider what it means. Introduce the word *riddle* and discuss the meaning. The children can now try to work out the answer. Read each clue carefully and ask the children to make suggestions.

● Reveal the answer, emphasising *ants* within *elephants*. (Pause for laughter, or groans, or incomprehension!) Re-read the poem, in the light of the answer. Ask the children for comments on the riddle (which they may link to familiar jokes). Ask them to share similar jokes or riddles they know.

● Ask the children to explain how the riddle (or joke) works, noting the word within the word and the absurdity of ants doing these things.

● Consider the form of the riddle. What features identify it as a poem? Note the rhymes, short lines and repetitions – features common in poetry.

● Ask the children to highlight the rhymes and note the range of spellings for the same sound.

● Focus on punctuation, noting the question marks. Note that the poem is in fact a series of questions, all beginning with *What kind of...?* Revise the spelling of *wh* question words. (You might also take the opportunity to revise *ph* in *elephant*.)

Activities

● Give the children some starting points for similar riddles – *lady<u>birds</u>, mon<u>keys</u>, trum<u>pets</u>, toad<u>stools</u>, mag<u>pies</u>, vege<u>tables</u>, mush<u>rooms</u>, dough<u>nuts</u>, ig<u>loos</u>*. Ask the children to look for the words within words. Choose one and ask the children to discuss facts about this animal/object. For example, monkeys are brown and furry, they live in the jungle, they swing in the trees, they eat fruit. Demonstrate how to split the word and model writing a question in the style of the poem – *What kind of keys are brown and furry?* Draw attention to the spelling of *what* and the question mark at the end. Ask the children to suggest the next question and scribe it. (It is not important to try to rhyme at this point; focus on the wordplay.) The children can now compose one or two more questions in the same style. Finish with a suitable teasing sentence.

● The children can write their own riddles in the same style, choosing from suggested alternatives. Pairs could share facts about the chosen animal/object, and write two or three questions. Provide a writing frame with sentence starters to support less able children. Encourage them to read aloud as they write, to check for sense and punctuation. The children can share their riddles with another pair. Can they work them out?

● Ask the children to illustrate the original, and their own poems, demonstrating the absurd images created.

● Give the children copies of the text with the rhyming words omitted. Ask them to complete the missing words, with the correct spelling. More able children might explore other words for riddles, beyond those suggested, using the dictionary if appropriate.

Extension/further reading

Collections of other poems by Tony Mitton (in a range of different forms, using language play and familiar settings) include *Big Bad Raps* (Orchard) and *Fluff and Other Stuff* (Orchard).

2: 3: T6: to read, respond imaginatively, recommend and collect examples of humorous stories, extracts, poems

2: 3: T8: to discuss meanings of words and phrases that create humour, and sound effects in poetry, e.g. nonsense poems, tongue-twisters, riddles, and to classify poems into simple types; to make class anthologies

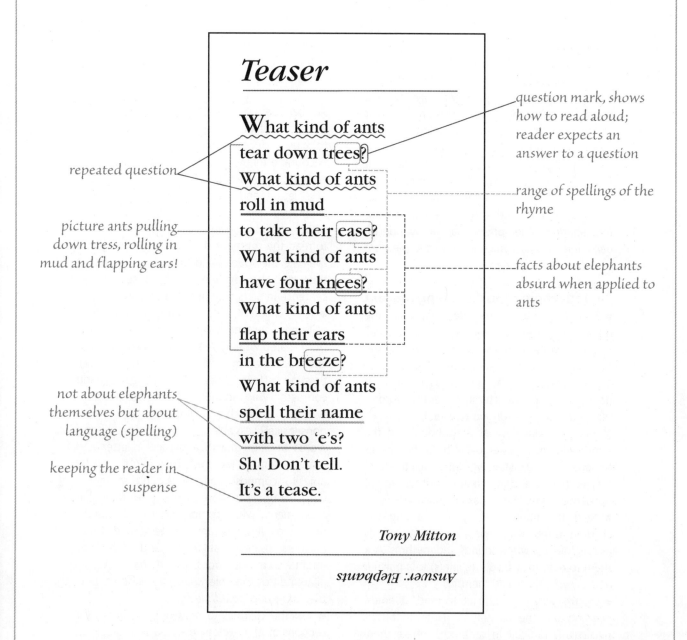

question mark, shows how to read aloud; reader expects an answer to a question

repeated question

range of spellings of the rhyme

picture ants pulling down tress, rolling in mud and flapping ears!

facts about elephants absurd when applied to ants

not about elephants themselves but about language (spelling)

keeping the reader in suspense

Teaser

What kind of ants
tear down trees?
What kind of ants
roll in mud
to take their ease?
What kind of ants
have four knees?
What kind of ants
flap their ears
in the breeze?
What kind of ants
spell their name
with two 'e's?
Sh! Don't tell.
It's a tease.

Tony Mitton

Answer: Elephants

2: 3: T11: to use humorous verse as a structure for children to write their own by adaptation, mimicry or substitution; to invent own riddles, language puzzles, jokes, nonsense sentences etc., derived from reading; write tongue-twisters or alliterative sentences; select words with care, re-reading and listening to their effect

2: 3: S6: to turn statements into questions, learning a range of 'wh' words typically used to open questions: *what, where, when, who* and to add question marks

Barry and Beryl the Bubble Gum Blowers
by Paul Cookson

Background

Tongue-twisters are phrases and sentences that rely on alliteration and are, therefore, difficult to read in a hurry. By their very nature, they are nonsense, since words are chosen for their sounds and not for sense or meaning. Children have always enjoyed the challenge of getting the words out as quickly as possible without stumbling. 'Barry and Beryl' is a tongue-twister in the form of a poem and, like all such verse, should be read aloud and at speed to savour the sounds. The poem has a wonderful galloping rhythm, which adds to the pleasure of the reading experience.

Shared reading and discussing the text

● Read and discuss the title. What will the poem be about? Will it be funny or serious? How can we tell? Ask the children to repeat the title more than once and notice the sounds.

● Read the poem, as quickly as possible. It doesn't matter if you stumble over the words – that is the point of tongue-twisters!

● Ask the children what they thought of the poem. What did they enjoy? Why? What makes the poem sound distinctive? Introduce the term *tongue-twister* and note that is another type of nonsense poem. What makes it nonsense?

● Read the poem line by line, asking the children to repeat the line after you, as quickly as possible. Enjoy the sounds and rhythms. Ask them to read their favourite line(s) to a partner and say why they liked them.

● Discuss why it is difficult to read at times, drawing out the alliteration. Note that it is particularly difficult in sentences where there are words beginning with *bl*.

● Ask the children what the rhythm sounds like, perhaps galloping horses or a train. Note how this drives the poem on at a great rate.

● How many 'b's can they find? Note that they appear in the middle of words as well as at the beginning. Which other letters are repeated? ('s' particularly.)

● Ask the children to highlight the rhyming words at the ends of lines. Encourage them to

enjoy the sounds of the words *balloons*, *baboons*, *bassoons*. Note the different spellings of *taste* and *traced*.

Activities

● Ask the children to suggest different letters to use for tongue-twisting sentences. Encourage them to repeat sounds to a partner and decide which sound interesting. Choose one letter and model composition of an alliterative sentence, such as *Slimy snails slithered slowly on the salad*. Ask the children to read the sentence several times quickly and evaluate the sounds and trickiness! You might then ask the children to compose another sentence in pairs, read it aloud and evaluate it.

● The children can compose their own alliterative sentences in pairs, using the models from shared writing. Ask them to read aloud to check for grammatical sense and for tongue-twisting effect. They can try several and compare. Which sounds make the best tongue-twisters? Which sentences are most nonsensical? Less able children could brainstorm words beginning with a particular letter and draw 'alliterative pictures'. They might then be able to compose tongue-twisting sentences with support. More able children can experiment with combinations of sounds, exploring digraphs and clusters, and tricky partnerships, such as *s*/*th*/*sh* and *bl*/*br*. They might also explore words that rhyme as well as alliterate (for example, *snake/shake/stake*, *pay/play/pray*, *bed/bread/bled*).

● Ask the children to read out the poem (or sections of it), developing speed with practice.

Extension/further reading

Compile an anthology of tongue-twisters to add to the collection of nonsense poems and other humorous verse. Paul Cookson has compiled collections of poems to be read aloud in *Unzip Your Lips* and *Who Rules the School?* (Macmillan). See tongue-twisters by McGough, King-Smith, Rosen, Foster and others in *The Puffin Book of Tongue Twisters*.

2: 3: T6: to read, respond imaginatively, recommend and collect examples of humorous stories, extracts, poems

2: 3: T8: to discuss meanings of words and phrases that create humour, and sound effects in poetry, e.g. nonsense poems, tongue-twisters, riddles, and to classify poems into simple types; to make class anthologies

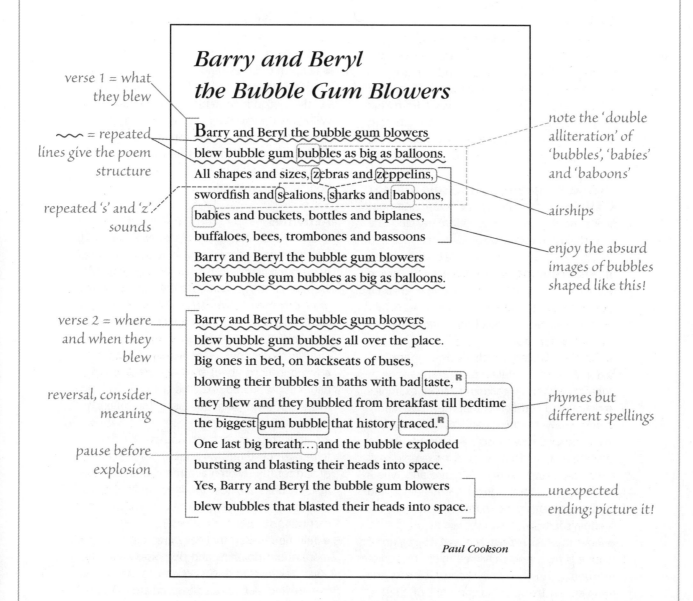

verse 1 = what they blew

∼∼ = repeated lines give the poem structure

repeated 's' and 'z' sounds

verse 2 = where and when they blew

reversal, consider meaning

pause before explosion

note the 'double alliteration' of 'bubbles', 'babies' and 'baboons'

airships

enjoy the absurd images of bubbles shaped like this!

rhymes but different spellings

unexpected ending; picture it!

Barry and Beryl the Bubble Gum Blowers

Barry and Beryl the bubble gum blowers
blew bubble gum bubbles as big as balloons.
All shapes and sizes, zebras and zeppelins,
swordfish and sealions, sharks and baboons,
babies and buckets, bottles and biplanes,
buffaloes, bees, trombones and bassoons
Barry and Beryl the bubble gum blowers
blew bubble gum bubbles as big as balloons.

Barry and Beryl the bubble gum blowers
blew bubble gum bubbles all over the place.
Big ones in bed, on backseats of buses,
blowing their bubbles in baths with bad taste,[R]
they blew and they bubbled from breakfast till bedtime
the biggest gum bubble that history traced.[R]
One last big breath… and the bubble exploded
bursting and blasting their heads into space.
Yes, Barry and Beryl the bubble gum blowers
blew bubbles that blasted their heads into space.

Paul Cookson

2: 3: T11: to use humorous verse as a structure for children to write their own by adaptation, mimicry or substitution; to invent own riddles, language puzzles, jokes, nonsense sentences etc., derived from reading; write tongue-twisters or alliterative sentences; select words with care, re-reading and listening to their effect

2: 3: S1: to read text aloud with intonation and expression appropriate to the grammar and punctuation

Fact or fiction?

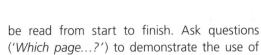

Background

These extracts are from the contents and index pages of a fiction and a non-fiction book (*The Otter Who Wanted to Know* and *The Book of Whales, Dolphins and Porpoises*). They will enable the children to build on work from Year 1, developing understanding of the different uses and purposes of fiction and non-fiction, and beginning to distinguish fact from fiction.

Shared reading and discussing the text

● If possible, have a range of fiction and non-fiction books on display. Before reading the text, discuss the difference between *fact* and *fiction*. Put the two words on the board and ask the children to discuss their meanings, giving definitions as appropriate. Give the children some statements and ask whether they are fact or fiction (some may be *opinions*; introduce this term if appropriate).

● Ask the children which kinds of book are fiction and which contain facts, using the term *non-fiction*. Ask the children to share examples of fiction and non-fiction that they have read.

● Now show the texts, and ask the children what they notice, discussing headings (in capitals), lists and numbers, for example. Ask them what kind of texts they are and where they might be found. Read the headings and discuss *contents* and *index* to establish the children's familiarity with the words.

● Read the first extract and ask what kind of book it is from (some children might recognise the book). How do they know? Discuss the numbers on the left and the right of the list, noting that they are *chapter* and page numbers, and are organised in the order in which they appear in the book. Consider how and when you might use a contents page in a fiction (story) book. Could you read just one chapter?

● Read the second extract and ask again about the kind of book it is from (and what the book is about), its use and purpose, noting again the numerical order. Draw out of the discussion the fact that non-fiction can be read by selecting particular pages or sections; it does not have to

be read from start to finish. Ask questions (*'Which page…?'*) to demonstrate the use of the contents.

● Read the index and discuss its use and purpose, noting that it is from the same book as the second contents page. Remind the children of earlier work on indexes (see page 70), and discuss their organisation. Note similarities and differences between index and contents pages and ask the children why a book might have both.

Activities

● Give the children a set of statements to sort into 'fact' or 'fiction', and ask them to consider how they know which is which. For example, *The magic key began to blow; Glow worms give off their own light*. Differentiate the reading level of the statements to be classified. You might include opinions for more able children to consider – fact, fiction or opinion?

● Set questions about the contents and index pages in the shared text. The children can then make up their own questions for others to answer.

● Cut up the three extracts and ask the children to reassemble them. Vary the size of the chunks of text for the children according to ability. Less able children can sort the index into sections, according to first letter. More able children can sort using second or third letter.

● Tell the children that they are going to read more about dolphins and porpoises (see page 104). Ask pairs to discuss one thing they would like to find out about these creatures. Write some questions on the board, reminding the children about the use and spelling of question words and question marks.

Extension/further reading

Give the children a selection of non-fiction texts and ask them to record their titles and whether they have a contents page, index and glossary (revising work done in Term 2). They could evaluate how easy it was to use each of these features in different books.

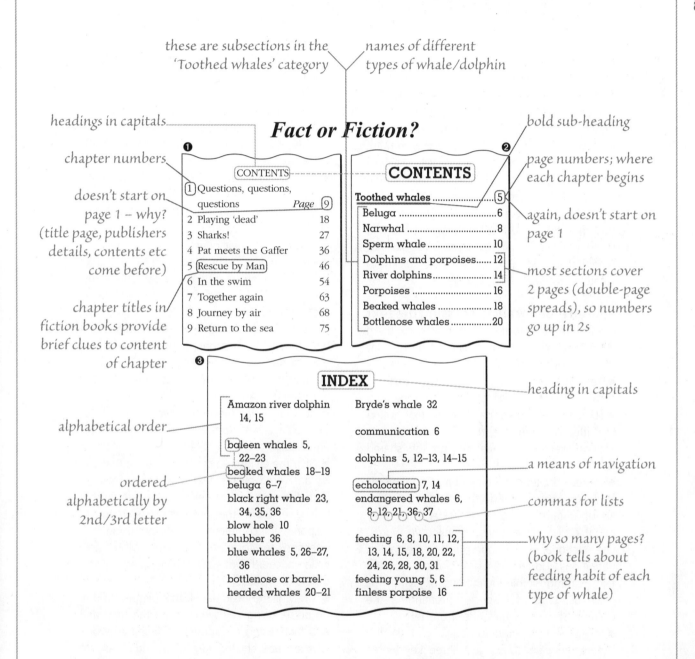

these are subsections in the 'Toothed whales' category

names of different types of whale/dolphin

headings in capitals

chapter numbers

doesn't start on page 1 – why? (title page, publishers details, contents etc come before)

chapter titles in fiction books provide brief clues to content of chapter

Fact or Fiction?

❶

CONTENTS

1 Questions, questions, questions   Page 9
2 Playing 'dead'   18
3 Sharks!   27
4 Pat meets the Gaffer   36
5 Rescue by Man   46
6 In the swim   54
7 Together again   63
8 Journey by air   68
9 Return to the sea   75

❷

CONTENTS

Toothed whales 5
Beluga 6
Narwhal 8
Sperm whale 10
Dolphins and porpoises...... 12
River dolphins..................... 14
Porpoises 16
Beaked whales 18
Bottlenose whales 20

bold sub-heading

page numbers; where each chapter begins

again, doesn't start on page 1

most sections cover 2 pages (double-page spreads), so numbers go up in 2s

❸

INDEX

Amazon river dolphin 14, 15

baleen whales 5, 22–23
beaked whales 18–19
beluga 6–7
black right whale 23, 34, 35, 36
blow hole 10
blubber 36
blue whales 5, 26–27, 36
bottlenose or barrel-headed whales 20–21

Bryde's whale 32

communication 6

dolphins 5, 12–13, 14–15

echolocation 7, 14
endangered whales 6, 8, 12, 21, 36, 37

feeding 6, 8, 10, 11, 12, 13, 14, 15, 18, 20, 22, 24, 26, 28, 30, 31
feeding young 5, 6
finless porpoise 16

alphabetical order

ordered alphabetically by 2nd/3rd letter

heading in capitals

a means of navigation

commas for lists

why so many pages? (book tells about feeding habit of each type of whale)

Dolphins and Porpoises

Background

This is an extract from *The Book of Whales, Dolphins and Porpoises*, from which the contents and index in the previous text were drawn. Children are often fascinated by these mammals, and many will be familiar with them from television programmes. The text is a non-chronological report and gives information about appearance, feeding habits and behaviour in simple language. Children can pose questions and look for answers; the text offers the opportunity to develop the skills of scanning – looking through a text quickly to locate information using key words.

Shared reading and discussing the text

● Show the text to the children and ask them what they think it is about. Is it fiction or non-fiction? How do they know?
● Read the text to the children. Ask pairs to discuss it and feed back one fact from the text.
● Look at the different parts of the text, noting the title, the main text, the illustration and its caption. Label these features on the shared text.
● Re-read the text, stopping at particular words to discuss meanings. Speculate and share ideas about unfamiliar words. Consider how they might find out meanings of unknown words. Use dictionaries as appropriate to establish definitions. Compile a class glossary for the text, writing simple definitions or synonyms (such as 'types' for *species*), reminding the children of work on glossaries from Term 2.
● Read the first paragraph again and ask the children in pairs to suggest three key words which show what it is about. Take some suggestions and highlight key words in the paragraph (such as *toothed whales, V-shaped flippers, curved fin, feed, fish, squid, octopuses, 31 species*). Repeat for the second and third paragraphs.
● Select one question from those generated during work on the previous text that can now be answered by using this extract. Demonstrate how to scan the text, looking for key words, to

decide which part might contain the answer. Think aloud as you scan, for example: *What do dolphins eat? So, I need to look for something about food or eating.* Answer the question, modelling how to use the question in the answer, for example: *What do dolphins eat? Dolphins eat…*
● Consider the other questions posed by the children. Can they all be answered from the text? If not, how might they find answers? How could they tell whether a non-fiction book would answer their questions? Show how the contents, index and headings can all be used to decide what information is in a particular text.

Activities

● Put an enlarged picture of the dolphin on the board. Read the first paragraph again and help the children underline key facts. Label the dolphin, using words that describe its appearance. Add further information to the picture as a factfile – *toothed whale, feeds on… 31 species*. Note how the key words only are used.
● Give the children a set of questions that can be answered by the text. Encourage them to scan the text for the relevant key words that will give them the answers. Ask them to respond in complete sentences, using the question to form the answer. More able children could write their own questions for others to answer.
● The children can label the picture of the porpoise, using key words from the text, and add facts using the model from shared work. Give less able children key words and phrases to match to the picture.

Extension/further reading

Ask the children to use other sources (books, CD-ROMs or the Internet) to find answers to questions not in this text. Encourage them to use contents, index and headings as appropriate to locate information. Give the children a range of other non-fiction books. Set questions that could be answered by using the books.

2: 3: T13: to understand the distinction between fact and fiction; to use terms 'fact', 'fiction' and 'non-fiction' appropriately

2: 3: T14: to pose questions and record these in writing, prior to reading non-fiction to find answers

large, bold heading

paragraph about dolphins

□ K = key words

paragraph about porpoises

mainly

problems associated with living near people

benefits for people

behaviour

sub-heading

caption

types

picture adds information to the text

inverted commas because they don't really talk

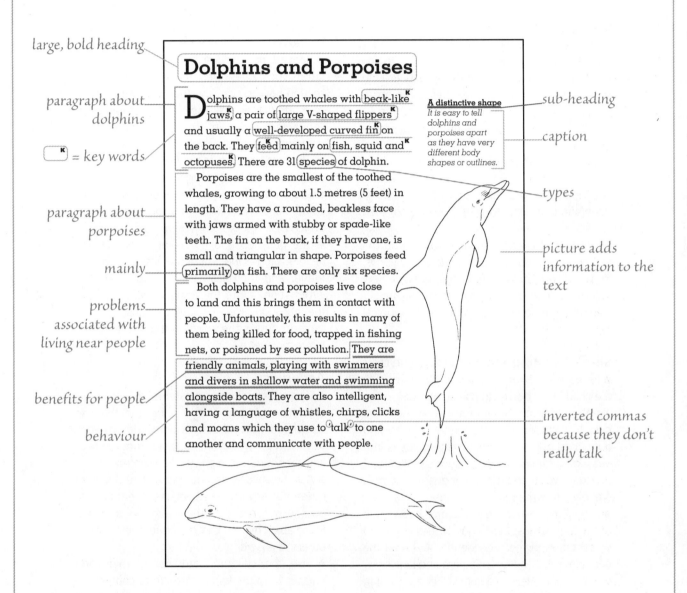

Dolphins and Porpoises

Dolphins are toothed whales with beak-like jaws, a pair of large V-shaped flippers and usually a well-developed curved fin on the back. They feed mainly on fish, squid and octopuses. There are 31 species of dolphin.

Porpoises are the smallest of the toothed whales, growing to about 1.5 metres (5 feet) in length. They have a rounded, beakless face with jaws armed with stubby or spade-like teeth. The fin on the back, if they have one, is small and triangular in shape. Porpoises feed primarily on fish. There are only six species.

Both dolphins and porpoises live close to land and this brings them in contact with people. Unfortunately, this results in many of them being killed for food, trapped in fishing nets, or poisoned by sea pollution. They are friendly animals, playing with swimmers and divers in shallow water and swimming alongside boats. They are also intelligent, having a language of whistles, chirps, clicks and moans which they use to 'talk' to one another and communicate with people.

A distinctive shape
It is easy to tell dolphins and porpoises apart as they have very different body shapes or outlines.

2: 3: T16: to scan a text to find specific sections, e.g. key words or phrases, sub-headings

2: 3: T17: to skim-read title, contents page, illustrations, chapter headings and sub-headings, to speculate what a book might be about

2: 3: T18: to evaluate the usefulness of a text for its purpose

Our Solar System

Background

Earth and space are fascinating topics for many children. This extract is an introduction to the solar system – the Sun and the objects around it. It demonstrates many features common to non-chronological reports – headings, sub-headings, diagrams and labels. It uses simple language, while introducing technical terminology, which is often explained within the text. Many children will bring previous knowledge to the text and will be able to generate questions to give purpose to their reading.

The text offers opportunities to develop the children's non-fiction reading and writing skills, in particular skimming (reading a passage very quickly to get an overview of its contents), leading to writing their own non-chronological reports.

Shared reading and discussing the text

● Introduce the topic – stars and planets. Ask the children to discuss in pairs what they know already and record this for future use. Ask them now to consider what they would like to find out. Demonstrate how to turn their ideas into questions, reminding them about spellings of question words and the use of question marks. Ask pairs to write three questions.

● Reveal the text and discuss prior knowledge of the term *solar system*. Look at the layout and presentation of the text. Identify and read the heading, sub-headings, diagram and labels.

● Read the text, demonstrating reading strategies, including syllabification for multi-syllabic words.

● Highlight technical vocabulary in the text, and discuss meanings. Note that many are actually explained in the text. Use dictionaries or other reference books to research and write definitions for terms not explained.

● Read each section again and ask the children to give one fact from each section as you read.

● Note and discuss particular vocabulary choices, such as *massive* (the Sun). Establish its meaning, and brainstorm synonyms. Discuss each and consider the effect of alternatives in the text. Why did the author choose *massive*?

● Remind the children of the use of capital letters for names. Demonstrate with the first section how to scan the text, without reading, to locate names. Ask the children to find other capitalised words in the text (including the diagram). List all the proper nouns found. You might note words that are not capitalised such as *planets* and *moons*.

● Select one of the questions posed earlier that can be answered from the text, for example *Which is the biggest planet?* Identify key words in the question and model how to skim the headings to decide where the answer might be found, and then scan the text to locate the information. Write the answer *Jupiter* next to the question. Now model the answer as a sentence, using the words in the question, *The biggest planet is...*

Activities

● Give the children questions that can be answered by using the text. Remind them to skim headings and scan text to find answers. Ask them to write a brief answer from the text, and then turn it into a complete sentence.

● Ask the children to find and write answers to questions they posed earlier. Ask them to note questions for which there are no answers. More able children can generate questions for others to answer from the text.

● Give the children cards with words and phrases from the text. Ask them to compete in pairs to locate the word or phrase and read the sentence. Differentiate the words and phrases to be located. Give less able children words from specific sections.

Extension/further reading

Research the Sun, the planets, asteroids and moons. Suitable non-fiction books include *3D Eyewitness: Space* by Richard Walker (Dorling Kindersley), *Stars and Planets* (Usborne Hotshots series) by M Ross and *Stars and Planets* by Maureen Hill (Brockhampton Press).

2: 3: T14: to pose questions and record these in writing, prior to reading non-fiction to find answers

2: 3: T16: to scan a text to find specific sections, e.g. key words or phrases, sub-headings

repetition to reinforce continuous movement

introduction of term 'solar system'

strong word

large sub-headings

technical term 'gravity' explained within text

capital letters for names (proper nouns)

choice of word, stronger than 'big'

called 'belt' because it goes all the way around the Sun

each section explains part of solar system

a hollow in surface caused by impact of a meteorite

scientists are not sure

diagram shows this information and relative distances from Sun

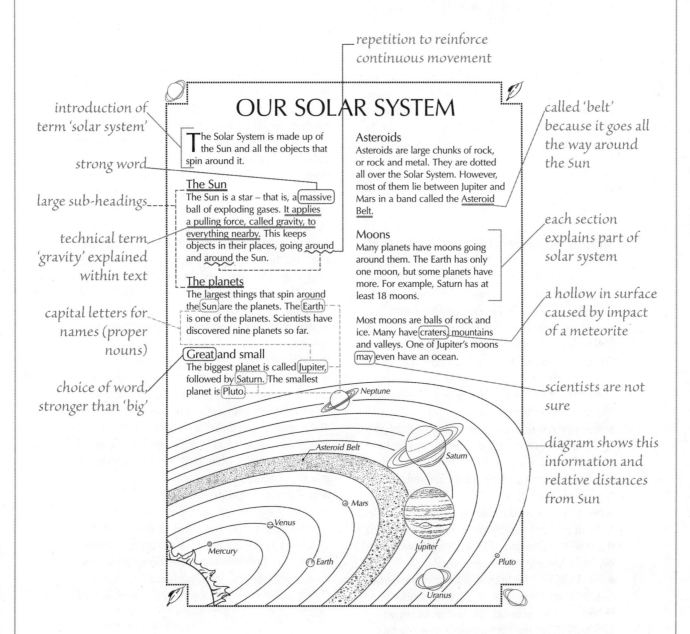

OUR SOLAR SYSTEM

The Solar System is made up of the Sun and all the objects that spin around it.

The Sun
The Sun is a star – that is, a massive ball of exploding gases. It applies a pulling force, called gravity, to everything nearby. This keeps objects in their places, going around and around the Sun.

The planets
The largest things that spin around the Sun are the planets. The Earth is one of the planets. Scientists have discovered nine planets so far.

Great and small
The biggest planet is called Jupiter, followed by Saturn. The smallest planet is Pluto.

Asteroids
Asteroids are large chunks of rock, or rock and metal. They are dotted all over the Solar System. However, most of them lie between Jupiter and Mars in a band called the Asteroid Belt.

Moons
Many planets have moons going around them. The Earth has only one moon, but some planets have more. For example, Saturn has at least 18 moons.

Most moons are balls of rock and ice. Many have craters, mountains and valleys. One of Jupiter's moons may even have an ocean.

Neptune

Asteroid Belt

Saturn

Mars

Venus

Mercury

Earth

Jupiter

Pluto

Uranus

2: 3: T19: to make simple notes from non-fiction texts, e.g. key words and phrases, page references, headings, to use in subsequent writing

2: 3: W10: to use synonyms and other alternative words/phrases that express same or similar meanings; to collect, discuss similarities and shades of meaning and use to extend and enhance writing

2: 3: S5: to write in clear sentences using capital letters and full stops accurately

Pushing and pulling

Background

This is a non-chronological report on a science topic likely to be covered in Year 2. It provides information on the topic in simple language, using illustrations and examples to clarify meaning. Children will be able to select key facts, perhaps drawing on work in science, to write their own non-chronological reports. The skills of skimming and scanning can be revised and consolidated.

Shared reading and discussing the text

● Tell the children that the text they are going to read is from a book called *Forces and Movement*. Read the title of the extract, referring to work in science if appropriate.

● Read the text with the children. Ask pairs to select three key words in the text. Share these and put them on the board. Discuss meanings of the words, noting that most are explained within the text. Use a dictionary to establish definitions where necessary.

● Ask the children to identify features of the layout that make the page interesting and help the reader. Make a class list to include headings/sub-headings (in small capitals for emphasis), illustration and caption.

● Remind the children how to get the main ideas of parts of text by skimming. Ask them to read the text again in pairs and decide what the key facts are and share some ideas.

● Read the first section. Ask the children what it tells you. Note that it is an introduction, telling the reader what the text is going to be about. Perhaps the first sentence is a key fact.

● Ask why *exerted* is in italic in the next paragraph. Discuss the meaning, if not already done so, noting that it is a key 'topic word' – scientific vocabulary. Remind them how to scan the text for other instances of the word.

Activities

● Focus on the paragraph beginning *Pushes and pulls…* Ask the children to explore forces, noting what happens when you push or pull and how you make things change direction or speed. This may be part of work on science. Share findings and make notes together.

● Tell the children they are going to make posters about forces. Explain that they need to be clear and simple. Discuss the title and model writing one or two introductory sentences, such as *There are two types of forces…* Re-read during writing to check for sense and punctuation. Draw attention to the present tense verb. Decide on headings, such as *Pushes, Pulls, Changing speed, Changing direction* and so on. Share ideas and write a sentence under the first heading. Ask pairs to write another sentence, perhaps on whiteboards. Choose one, discussing why you have chosen it, and write it up.

● The children can now continue writing under the headings identified. Remind them to use the class prompt list to organise and lay out their writing, incorporating illustrations and captions where appropriate. Less able children can work with support to compose as a group. They might be given a writing frame or a prepared piece of text with omitted words. Encourage more able children to include as much information as possible, giving examples and using appropriate vocabulary.

● Give the children a wordsearch of topic words. When they have found them, ask the children to compile personal glossaries of topic words, writing simple definitions. Use the words for spelling and handwriting practice. Give less able children words and definitions to match, to compile a glossary.

Extension/further reading

Ask the children to consider what else they would like to know about forces and write questions. Give them a selection of books, for example *Forces* by Robert Snedden (Heinemann) and *Forces and Motion* by Peter Riley (Heinemann). Ask them to select books by using contents, index and headings in order to find answers to their questions. They can make notes from the text, which can be turned into sentences.

2: 3: T16: to scan a text to find specific sections, e.g. key words or phrases, sub-headings

2: 3: T19: to make simple notes from non-fiction texts, e.g. key words and phrases, page references, headings, to use in subsequent writing

K = key words

key fact; 1st sentence to emphasise importance

present tense verbs for non-chronological reports

sub-headings large and in small capitals

in italic – key word, scientific vocabulary

examples to illustrate meaning of word

PUSHING AND PULLING

A [force]ᴷ is a [push]ᴷ or a [pull.]ᴷ You cannot see a force, but you can see and feel its effects. You [see] the effect of the wind's force as leaves move on a tree, or [feel] its effect as the air pushes against your skin.

EXERTING FORCES

The word [exerted] is used to describe how a force is made. We say that the wind exerts a force when it blows the leaves. You exert a force on this page when you hold it.

Pushes and pulls move things. Once something is moving, a pull or a push may be exerted to change its direction and speed – or to stop it altogether. For example, you may use a bat to change the direction of a ball that is thrown to you.

The force of the wind is making these trees bend.

captions for pictures in italic to emphasise they are captions and not part of main text

These children are using their muscles, exerting a force to pick up these containers.

MOVEMENT
Without forces there would be no movement. When muscles work, they exert forces that pull on your bones and move your [limbs,] letting you run, walk and swim. Engines exert forces to move cars, trucks, ships, submarines and spacecraft.

legs and arms

pictures bring subject to life and make it more accessible – real children lifting real object

2: 3: T21: to write non-chronological reports based on structure of known texts, e.g. *There are two sorts of x...; They live in x...; the A's have x...; but the B's etc.*, using appropriate language to present, sequence and categorise ideas.

2: 3: W9: new words from reading linked to particular topics, to build individual collections of personal interest or significant words

But you promised!

...I could have a pet

"But you *promised* I could have a pet," wailed Kitty.

"No I didn't," said Mum firmly. "Not a proper promise. I just said…"

"You said I could have a dog for Christmas – you DID!"

Kitty was cross and disappointed. Mum and Dad had said she could have a pet for Christmas, and she and Daniel had decided a dog would be most fun. But now Mum had a job, and so she said it would be too much trouble. "I'll have so much to do, Kitty," she sighed. "You must understand."

But Kitty only understood one thing. "You *said* we'd get a dog, and Dad said he'd like one too, didn't you Dad?"

"Well, yes, I did," said Dad.

"I want us to have a pet. All the boys in school have animals. And I'd help Kitty look after it," said Daniel.

"But puppies need training, and dogs have to be taken for walks, and dog food has to be bought – and who'd do all that?" asked Mum. "I wanted this job so much, and it means I'll have less time to do all the things I have to do."

"What about a little kitten?" asked Kitty, in a small voice.

"I don't want extra chores," said Mum firmly. "I'm sorry." She sounded cross, but a bit guilty too.

Kitty looked furious.

Dan looked disappointed.

"Oh dear," said Dad.

Kitty turned and ran from the room, not minding that she made all the decorations on the tree shiver as she passed. Up in her room she picked up Mr Tubs and hugged him. "Grown-ups *never* keep their promises," she whispered. "So it looks as if we won't get our puppy, Mr T."

Bel Mooney

A List

One morning Toad sat in bed.

"I have many things to do," he said. "I will write them all down on a list so that I can remember them."

Toad wrote on a piece of paper:

A list of things to do today

Then he wrote:

Wake up

"I have done that," said Toad, and he crossed out:

Wake up

Then Toad wrote other things on the paper.

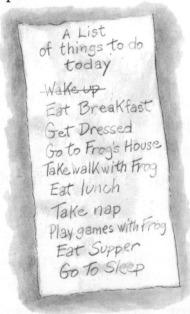

"There," said Toad. "Now my day is all written down."

He got out of bed and had something to eat. Then Toad crossed out:

Eat Breakfast

Toad took his clothes out of the cupboard and put them on. Then he crossed out:

Get Dressed

Toad put the list in his pocket. He opened the door and walked out into the morning. Soon Toad was at Frog's front door. He took the list from his pocket and crossed out:

Go to Frog's House

Toad knocked at the door.

"Hello," said Frog.

"Look at my list of things to do," said Toad.

"Oh," said Frog, "that is very nice."

Toad said, "My list tells my that we will go for a walk."

"All right," said Frog. "I am ready."

Frog and Toad went on a long walk. Then Toad took the list from his pocket again. He crossed out:

Take walk with Frog

Just then there was a strong wind. It blew the list out of Toad's hand. The list blew high up into the air.

"Help!" cried Toad. "My list is blowing away. What will I do without my list?"

Illustration and text © Arnold Lobel

The Rare Spotted Birthday Party

"I feel a bit sick," said Mark. "Even if I *could* have a birthday, I don't think I would want it."

"That's the worst thing," said Sarah. "Not even *wanting* a birthday is worst of all."

Two days later, when the birthday really came, Mark did not feel sick any more. He just felt spotty.

He opened his presents at breakfast.

His mother and father had given him a camera. It was small, but it would take real pictures. Sarah gave him a paint box. (She always gave him a paint box. Whenever Mark got a new paint box, he gave Sarah the old one.)

All morning they painted.

"It feels funny today," said Mark. "It doesn't feel like a birthday. It doesn't feel special at all."

Sarah had painted a class of children. Now she began to paint spots on them.

Lunch was plain and healthy.

In the afternoon Mark's mother started to brush him all over. She brushed his hair. She brushed his dressing gown, though it was new and didn't need brushing. She brushed his slippers.

"We will have a birthday drive," she said. "The car windows will stop the measles from getting out."

They drove out into the country and up a hill that Mark knew. "There's Peter's house," he said. "Peter-up-the-hill! He has measles, too."

"We might pay him a visit for a moment," Mark's mother said. "He won't catch measles from you if he has them already."

The front door was open. They rang the bell and walked in. Then Mark got a real surprise! The room was full of people. Lots of the people were boys wearing dressing-gowns – all of them spotty boys, MEASLE-Y boys.

"Happy birthday! Happy birthday!" they shouted.

Margaret Mahy

THE MAGIC FINGER

For months I had been telling myself that I would never put the Magic Finger upon anyone again – not after what happened to my teacher, old Mrs Winter.

Poor old Mrs Winter.

One day we were in class, and she was teaching us spelling. "Stand up," she said to me, "and spell cat."

"That's an easy one," I said. "*K-a-t.*"

"You are a stupid little girl!" Mrs Winter said.

"I am not a stupid little girl!" I cried. "I am a very nice little girl!"

"Go and stand in the corner," Mrs Winter said.

Then I got cross, and I saw red, and I put the Magic Finger on Mrs Winter good and strong, and almost at once…

Guess what?

Whiskers began growing out of her face! They were long black whiskers, just like the ones you see on a cat, only much bigger. And how fast they grew! Before we had time to think, they were out to her ears!

Of course the whole class started screaming with laughter, and then Mrs Winter said, "Will you be so kind as to tell me what you find so madly funny, all of you?"

And when she turned around to write something on the blackboard we saw that she had grown a *tail* as well! It was a huge bushy tail!

I cannot begin to tell you what happened after that, but if any of you are wondering whether Mrs Winter is quite all right again now, the answer is No. And she never will be.

Roald Dahl

The Werepuppy

"I'm going to have a smashing summer, Miss Monk," said Micky. "I'm going to take Wolfie to the park every day."

The last time Micky had taken him to the park, Wolfie had picked a fight with every dog in sight, barked hysterically at the ducks on the pond, and snatched an ice-cream from a small child's hand and swallowed it in one gulp. The ice-cream, not the hand. Wolfie was actually quite gentle with most little children. Apart from Marigold.

"I'm going to spend the summer getting Wolfie to obey all my orders," said Micky, with unreasonable optimism.

Mum brought Wolfie with her when she came to meet Micky and Marigold when school broke up. Wolfie came flying across the playground, his teeth bared in a great grin, his grey fur sticking up spikily.

Most of the children laughed and pointed. Some stepped back rather rapidly out of Wolfie's way. Darren Smith just happened to be bending down, doing up his Doc Martens. Wolfie spotted him and his grin grew wider. He decided to try out a goat imitation. He lowered his head and charged. Wolfie butted Darren right on the bottom and sent him flying.

Darren wasn't hurt. Just his dignity. Everyone laughed at him. Micky practically fell about, and Wolfie gave short sharp barks as if he was snorting with laughter too.

Darren didn't find it funny at all.

"That mangy old dog ought to be put down!" he yelled. "You keep it away from me, Micky."

"I think it's certainly about time you got your dog trained, Micky," said Miss Monk, crossing the playground.

"He can be quite good sometimes, honestly, Miss," said Micky.

And as if to prove his point Wolfie wiped his paws on the sprawling Darren Smith and trotted meekly up to Miss Monk, head a little bowed, as if overcome by her presence.

Jacqueline Wilson

I'm not scared of the monster

I'm not scared of the monster
That hides beneath my bed.
When it leaps out
To prowl about,
I pat it on the head.

I'm not scared of the monster
That lurks behind the door.
When it leaps out
To prowl about,
I shake its furry paw.

I'm not scared of the monster
That skulks under the chair.
When it leaps out
To prowl about,
I stroke its spiky hair.

I'm not scared of the monsters,
'Cause they're no longer there.
When I leapt out
To scream and shout,
I gave them all a scare!

John Foster

Don't

Don't do this, don't do that.
Don't scrape your plate.
Don't tease the cat.
Don't pick your nose.
Don't suck your thumb.
Don't scratch your head.
Don't swallow gum.
Don't stick your tongue out.
Don't make that face at me.
Don't wear your socks in bed.
Don't slurp your tea.
Don't touch your father's records.
Don't touch your brother's glue.

So many things I *mustn't* —
Whatever *can* I do?

John Kitching

DINNER-TIME RHYME

Can you tell me, if you please,
Who it is likes mushy peas?
    Louise likes peas.
How about Sam?
    Sam likes Spam.
How about Vince?
    Vince likes mince.
How about Kelly?
    Kelly likes jelly.
How about Trish?
    Trish likes fish.
How about Pips?
    Pips likes chips.
How about Pete?
    Pete likes meat.
How about Sue?
    Sue likes stew.
How about Greg?
    Greg likes egg.
How about Pam?
    Pam likes lamb.

OK, then, tell me, if you can –
How about Katerina Wilhelmina Theodora Dobson?

    She goes home for dinner…

June Crebbin

Best Friends

Would a best friend
   Eat your last sweet
   Talk about you behind your back
   Have a party and not ask you?

Mine did.

Would a best friend
   Borrow your bike without telling you
   Deliberately forget your birthday
   Avoid you whenever possible?

Mine did.

Would a best friend
   Turn up on your bike
   Give you a whole packet of your favourite sweets
   Look you in the eye?

Mine did.

Would a best friend say
   Sorry I talked about you behind your back
   Sorry I had a party and didn't invite you
   Sorry I deliberately forgot your birthday
   – I thought you'd fallen out with me.

Mine did.

And would a best friend say, simply,
  Never mind
  That's OK.

I did.

Bernard Young

What is the sun?

The sun is an orange dinghy
    sailing across a calm sea.

It is a gold coin
    dropped down a drain in Heaven.

It is a yellow beach ball
    kicked high into the summer sky.

It is a red thumb-print
    on a sheet of pale blue paper.

It is a milk bottle's gold top
    floating in a puddle.

Wes Magee

DAD

Dad is the dancing-man
The laughing-bear, the prickle-chin,
The tickle-fingers, jungle-roars
Bucking bronco, rocking-horse,
The helicopter roundabout
The beat-the-wind at swing-and-shout
Goal-post, scarey-ghost
Climbing-Jack, humpty-back.

But sometimes he's
A go-away-please!
A snorey-snarl, a sprawly slump
A yawny mouth, a sleeping lump,

And I'm a kite without a string
Waiting for Dad to dance again.

Berlie Doherty

Chewy Chocolate Crunch Cakes

Makes 16 cakes

What you need:

Ingredients
375g plain chocolate
175g unsalted butter
250g puffed wheat
50g golden syrup

Equipment
1 saucepan
1 wooden spoon
16 paper cake cases
1 tablespoon
Weighing scales

What to do:

1. Break the chocolate into small pieces.

2. Put the chocolate into the saucepan with the butter and the syrup.

3. Heat the chocolate, butter and syrup gently until they are melted.

4. Take the pan off the heat.

5. Stir in the puffed wheat.

6. Put 1 tablespoon of the mixture into each cake case.

7. Leave until cold.

8. Share them with your friends!

Sue Taylor

The concertina book

1. Lay paper in front of you in the landscape position.

2. Fold vertically in half.

3. Then fold horizontally in half.

4. Open the crease you have just made.

5. Now fold vertically in half.

6. Open up the whole sheet.

7. Fold horizontally in half.

8. Zig-zag panels to make concertina book.

Paul Johnson

Following directions

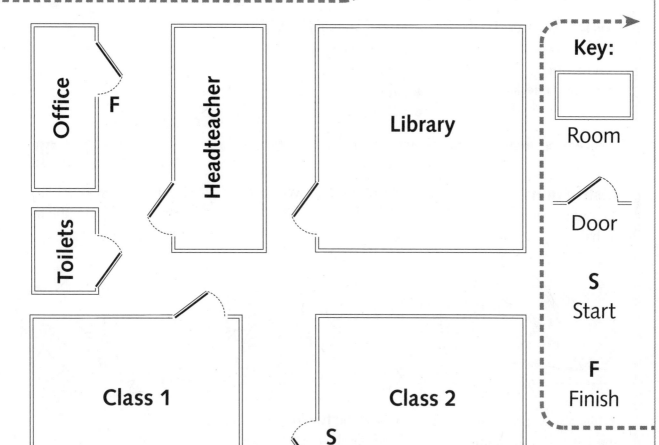

Key:

Room

Door

S
Start

F
Finish

How to get to the office from Class 2

First, go out of the door and turn right.

Then, walk along the corridor towards the library.

At the library, turn left.

Walk past Class 1.

When you get to the toilets, turn right.

Next, walk past the headteacher's room

Finally, turn left and knock on the office door.

Sue Taylor

Felt finger puppets

What you need:
- piece of felt (approx 14cm x 8cm)
- sewing needle
- cotton thread
- collage materials (wool, buttons, sequins)
- scissors
- glue
- felt pens

Instructions:

1. Fold the piece of felt in half.

2. Place your finger on the felt and draw a line around it.

3. Draw another line 2cm from the first line. Try to keep the same shape. This will be the cutting line.

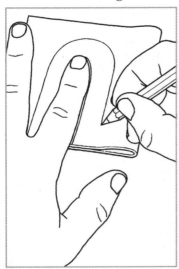

4. Cut out the two layers of fabric.

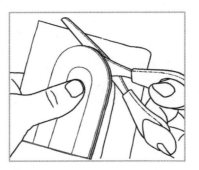

5. Sew the two pieces together. Leave the base edge free for your finger.

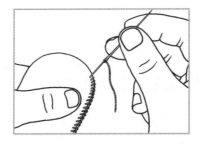

6. Turn the fabric so that the seams are inside.

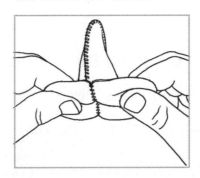

7. Stick or sew on collage materials to make the face and hair.

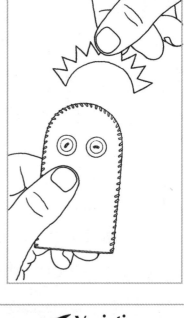

Variations

Josie McKinnon

50 Shared texts ● Year 2

HOW TO PLAY BOXES

This game will keep you amused for hours on a rainy day!

What you need:
- Sheets of paper (squared paper is best)
- 2 pencils or pens in different colours
- A friend to play with

How to play:

1. Draw a grid of dots on a piece of paper. Start with five lines of five dots and use a bigger grid next time if you enjoy the game.

3. If your line completes a square, write your initials in the square and have another turn. The game ends when all the squares are complete.

2. Take it in turns to join two dots with a line, horizontally or vertically, not diagonally.

4. The winner is the person with the most squares. JT has 9 squares, DT has 7 squares. JT is the winner!

Have fun!

Little Red Riding Hood *Extract 1*

There was once a little girl whose mother made her a new cloak with a hood. It was a lovely red colour and she liked to wear it so much that everyone called her Little Red Riding Hood.

One day her mother said to her, "I want you to take this basket of cakes to your grandmother who is ill."

Little Red Riding Hood liked to walk through the woods to her grandmother's cottage and she quickly put on her cloak. As she was leaving, her mother said, "Now remember, don't talk to any strangers on the way."

But Little Red Riding Hood loved talking to people, and as she was walking along the path, she met a wolf.

"Good morning, Little Girl, where are you off to in your beautiful red cloak?" said the wolf with a wicked smile.

Little Red Riding Hood put down her basket and said, "I'm taking some cakes to my grandmother who's not very well."

"Where does your grandmother live?" asked the wolf.

"In the cottage at the end of this path," said Little Red Riding Hood.

Now the wolf was really very hungry and he wanted to eat Little Red Riding Hood then and there. But he heard a woodcutter not far away and he ran off.

He went straight to the grandmother's cottage where he found the old woman sitting up in bed. Before she knew what was happening, he ate her up in one gulp. Then he put on the grandmother's nightdress and her nightcap, and climbed into her bed. He snuggled well down under the bedclothes and tried to hide himself.

Retold by Helen Oxenbury

Little Red Riding Hood *Extract 2*

Before long, Little Red Riding Hood came to the door with her basket of cakes and knocked.

"Come in," said the wolf, trying to make his voice sound soft.

At first, when she went in, Little Red Riding Hood thought that her grandmother must have a bad cold.

She went over to the bed. "What big eyes you have, Grandmama," she said, as the wolf peered at her from under the nightcap.

"All the better to see you with, my dear," said the wolf.

"What big ears you have, Grandmama."

"All the better to hear you with, my dear," said the wolf.

Then Little Red Riding Hood saw a long nose and a wide-open mouth. She wanted to scream but she said, very bravely, "What a big mouth you have, Grandmama."

At this the wolf opened his jaws wide. "All the better to eat you with!" he cried. And he jumped out of bed and ate up Little Red Riding Hood.

Just at that moment the woodcutter passed by the cottage. Noticing that the door was open, he went inside. When he saw the wolf he quickly swung his axe and chopped off his head.

Little Red Riding Hood and then her grandmother stepped out, none the worse for their adventure.

Little Red Riding Hood thanked the woodcutter and ran home to tell her mother all that had happened. And after that day, she never, ever, spoke to strangers.

Retold by Helen Oxenbury

BRER RABBIT AND THE TAR BABY

Extract 1

BRER FOX TOOK his Tar Baby down to the road, the very road Brer Rabbit walked along every morning. He sat the Tar Baby in the road, put a hat on it, and then hid in a ditch.

He had scarcely gotten comfortable (as comfortable as one can get in a ditch), before Brer Rabbit came strutting along like he owned the world and was collecting rent from everybody in it.

Seeing the Tar Baby, Brer Rabbit tipped his hat. "Good morning! Nice day, ain't it? Of course, any day I wake up and find I'm still alive is a nice day as far as I'm concerned." He laughed at his joke, which he thought was pretty good. (Ain't too bad if I say so myself.)

Tar Baby don't say a word. Brer Fox stuck his head up out of the ditch, grinning.

"You deaf?" Brer Rabbit asked the Tar Baby. "If you are, I can talk louder." He yelled, _"How you this morning? Nice day, ain't it?"_

Tar Baby still don't say nothing.

Brer Rabbit was getting kinna annoyed. "I don't know what's wrong with this young generation. Didn't your parents teach you no manners?"

Tar Baby don't say nothing.

"Well, I reckon I'll teach you some!" He hauls off and hits the Tar Baby. BIP! And his fist was stuck to the side of the Tar Baby's face.

"You let me go!" Brer Rabbit yelled. "Let me go or I'll really pop you one." He twisted and turned, but he couldn't get loose. "All right! I warned you!" And he smacked the Tar Baby on the other side of the head. BIP! His other fist was stuck.

Retold by Julius Lester

BRER RABBIT AND THE TAR BABY

Extract 2

"I guess I'm going to be barbecued this day." Brer Rabbit sighed. "But getting barbecued is a whole lot better than getting thrown in the briar patch." He sighed again. "No doubt about it. Getting barbecued is almost a blessing compared to being thrown into that briar patch on the other side of the road. If you got to go, go in a barbecue sauce. That's what I always say. How much lemon juice and brown sugar you put in yours?"

When Brer Fox heard this, he had to do some more thinking, because he wanted the worst death possible for that rabbit. "Now that I thinks on it, it's too hot to be standing over a hot fire. I think I'll hang you."

Brer Rabbit shuddered. "Hanging is a terrible way to die! Just terrible! But I thank you for being so considerate. Hanging is better than being thrown in the briar patch."

Brer Fox thought that over a minute. "Come to think of it, I can't hang you, 'cause I didn't bring my rope. I'll drown you in the creek over yonder."

Brer Rabbit sniffed like he was about to cry. "No, no, Brer Fox. You know I can't stand water, but I guess drowning, awful as it is, is better than the briar patch."

"I got it!" Brer Fox exclaimed. "I don't feel like dragging you all the way down to the creek. I got my knife right here. I'm going to skin you!" He pulled out his knife.

Retold by Julius Lester

RABBIT AND TIGER

Now Tiger was determined to kill Konehu the rabbit, so day after day she roamed the forest looking for him.

One day she spotted the rabbit high, high up on a rock gazing into the forest pool below. The yellow sun overhead, reflected in the water, looked like a golden ball.

"Konehu, Konehu, I am coming to kill you!" roared Tiger.

"Oh Tiger, you are just in time to witness a wonderful sight," said Konehu.

Tiger climbed right up to the rock where Konehu sat.

"What are you looking at?" asked Tiger.

"See that golden ball in the pool?" said Konehu. "If only we could get it out we would be richer than the King."

Tiger looked down at the golden ball. It was so bright that it lit up the water in the pool.

"Konehu," she said, "you are too small to lift such a large ball. Let me go in and bring it up for you."

Tiger intended to run off with the gold and keep it all for herself.

"Very well," said Konehu, "but when you get it, hold it fast. Don't let it slip from you or it will go deeper."

Quickly Tiger dived into the pool, but she came up spluttering and snorting. She had not found the gold.

Konehu called to her:

"Tiger my friend, be brave, be bold.
Go deep and deep to find the gold."

So once more Tiger dived down, down into the pool, into the cool water, and once more Tiger rose puffing and blowing so hard that she sprayed Konehu where he sat high up on the rock.

Tiger was ready to give up the search, but Konehu shouted:

"Tiger, you must be brave and bold.
Go deeper still to find the gold."

Retold by Grace Hallworth

Term 2: Traditional stories with predictable and patterned language

The Little Red Hen and the Grain of Wheat

One day as the Little Red Hen was scratching in a field, she found a grain of wheat.

"This wheat should be planted," she said. "Who will plant this grain of wheat?"

"Not I," said the Duck.

"Not I," said the Cat.

"Not I," said the Dog.

"Then I will," said the Little Red Hen. And she did.

Soon the wheat grew to be tall and yellow.

"The wheat is ripe," said the Little Red Hen. "Who will cut the wheat?"

"Not I," said the Duck.

"Not I," said the Cat.

"Not I," said the Dog.

"Then I will," said the Little Red Hen. And she did.

When the wheat was cut, the Little Red Hen said, "Who will thresh this wheat?"

"Not I," said the Duck.

"Not I," said the Cat.

"Not I," said the Dog.

"Then I will," said the Little Red Hen. And she did.

When the wheat was all threshed, the Little Red Hen said, "Who will take this wheat to the mill?"

"Not I," said the Duck.

"Not I," said the Cat.

"Not I," said the Dog.

"Then I will," said the Little Red Hen. And she did.

She took the wheat to the mill and had it ground into flour. Then she said, "Who will make this flour into bread?"

"Not I," said the Duck.

"Not I," said the Cat.

"Not I," said the Dog.

"Then I will," said the Little Red Hen. And she did.

She made and baked the bread. Then she said, "Who will eat this bread?"

"Oh! I will," said the Duck.

"And I will," said the Cat.

"And I will," said the Dog.

"No, No!" said the Little Red Hen. "I will do that."

And she did.

Retold by Sara Cone Bryant

Come-day Go-day

Here comes Monday.
School has begun day.
It's a hit-and-run day.
What a very glum day.
There goes Monday.

Here comes Tuesday.
Chase away the blues day.
You can pick and choose day.
Let's have a snooze day.
There goes Tuesday.

Here comes Wednesday.
Tying up the ends day.
It's a let's pretends day.
Drive you round the bends day.
There goes Wednesday.

Here comes Thursday.
It's a his and hers day.
Seen and not heard day.
Quite a connoisseur's day.
There goes Thursday.

Here comes Friday.
Knocks you sky-high day.
Sing a lullaby day.
Get some shuteye day.
There goes Friday.

Here comes Saturday.
Let's have a natter day.
Run and scatter day.
Mad as a hatter day.
There goes Saturday.

Here comes Sunday.
Meat overdone day.
Let's have some fun day.
Forget about Monday.
There goes Sunday.

Barrie Wade

Poem 1

The End

When I was One,
I had just begun.

When I was Two,
I was nearly new.

When I was Three,
I was hardly Me.

When I was Four,
I was not much more.

When I was Five,
I was just alive.

But now I am Six, I'm as clever as clever.
So I think I'll be six now for ever and ever.

AA Milne

Poem 2

Happiness

John had
Great Big
Waterproof
Boots on;
John had a
Great Big
Waterproof
Hat;
John had a
Great Big
Waterproof
Mackintosh –
And that
(Said John)
  Is
  That.

AA Milne

Morning

Morning comes
with a milk-float jiggling

Morning comes
with a milkman whistling

Morning comes
with empties clinking

Morning comes
with alarm-clock ringing

Morning comes
with toaster popping

Morning comes
with letters dropping

Morning comes
with kettle singing

Morning comes
with me just listening

Morning comes to drag me out of bed
— Boss-Woman Morning.

Grace Nichols

Caribbean Counting Rhyme

One by one
one by one
waves are dancing
in the sun.

Two by two
two by two
seashells pink
and purply-blue.

Three by three
three by three
big boats
putting out to sea.

Four by four
four by four
children fishing
on the shore.

Five by five
five by five
little walking
fish arrive.

Six by six
six by six
pelicans
performing tricks.

Seven by seven
seven by seven
puffy clouds
patrolling heaven.

Eight by eight
eight by eight
fishes nibbling
juicy bait.

Nine by nine
nine by nine
taking home
a catch that's fine.

Ten by ten
ten by ten
tomorrow we
will come again.

Pamela Mordecai

Word of a Lie

I am the fastest runner in my school and that's
NO WORD OF A LIE
I've got gold fillings in my teeth and that's
NO WORD OF A LIE
In my garden, I've got my own big bull and that's
NO WORD OF A LIE
I'm brilliant at giving my enemies grief and that's
NO WORD OF A LIE
I can multiply three billion and twenty-seven by nine billion four
    thousand and one in two seconds and that's
NO WORD OF A LIE
I can calculate the distance between planets before you've had
    toast and that's
NO WORD OF A LIE
I can always tell when my best pals boast and that's
NO WORD OF A LIE
I'd been round the world twice before I was three and a quarter
    and that's
NO WORD OF A LIE
I am definitely my mother's favourite daughter and that's
NO WORD OF A LIE
I am brilliant at fake laughter. I go Ha aha Ha ha ha and that's
NO WORD OF A LIE
I can tell the weather from one look at the sky and that's
NO WORD OF A LIE
I can predict disasters, floods, earthquakes and murders and that's
NO WORD OF A LIE
I can always tell when other people lie and that's
NO WORD OF A LIE
I can even tell if someone is going to die and that's
NO WORD OF A LIE
I am the most popular girl in my entire school and that's
NO WORD OF A LIE
I know the golden rule, don't play the fool, don't boast, be shy and
    that's
NO WORD OF A LIE
I am sensitive, I listen, I have kind brown eyes and that's
NO WORD OF A LIE

You don't believe me do you?
ALL RIGHT, ALL RIGHT, ALL RIGHT
I am the biggest liar in my school and that's
NO WORD OF A LIE

Jackie Kay

Conversation

I'm just going out for a moment.
Why?
To make a cup of tea.
Why?
Because I'm thirsty.
Why?
Because it's hot.
Why?
Because the sun is shining.
Why?
Because it's summer.
Why?
Because that's when it is.
Why?
Why don't you stop saying why?
Why?
Tea-time. That's why.
High-time-you-stopped-saying-why-time.
What?

Michael Rosen

Dictionary entries

undo

a b c d e f g h i j k l m n o p q r s t **Uu** v w x y z

undo undoes, undoing, undid, undone
VERB If you **undo** something that is tied up, you untie it.

undress undresses, undressing, undressed
VERB When you **undress**, you take off your clothes.

uneasy
ADJECTIVE If you are **uneasy**, you are worried that something is wrong.

unemployed
ADJECTIVE Someone who is **unemployed** does not have a job.

uneven
ADJECTIVE Something that is **uneven** does not have a flat, smooth surface.

unexpected
ADJECTIVE Something that is **unexpected** surprises you.
unexpectedly adverb

unfair
ADJECTIVE If you think that something is **unfair**, it does not seem right or reasonable to you.
unfairly ADVERB

unfortunate
ADJECTIVE **1** Someone who is **unfortunate** is unlucky.
ADJECTIVE **2** If you say something is **unfortunate**, you mean you wish it had not happened.
unfortunately ADVERB

unfriendly
ADJECTIVE Someone who is **unfriendly** is not kind to you.

ungrateful
ADJECTIVE If someone is **ungrateful**, they are not thankful for something that has been given to them or done for them.

unhappy unhappier, unhappiest
ADJECTIVE Someone who is **unhappy** is sad or miserable.
unhappily ADVERB

unhealthy unhealthier, unhealthiest
ADJECTIVE **1** Someone who is **unhealthy** is often ill.
ADJECTIVE **2** Something that is **unhealthy** is likely to cause illness.

Synonyms

Synonyms are words that have the same, or almost the same, meaning. Here are some useful synonyms for everyday words.

angry
furious, mad, annoyed,
outraged, indignant

bad
a bad person – wicked, nasty
a bad child – naughty,
spiteful, defiant
bad food – rotten, decayed
a bad pain – severe
bad news – distressing,
grave, terrible

big
huge, large, enormous,
gigantic, vast, colossal

good
a good dog – well-behaved
a good painting – fine
a good film – enjoyable
a good worker – able, clever

happy
cheerful, contented, delighted,
glad, pleased, thrilled

kind
kind of person or thing – type,
class, group

level
grade, position, stage

lots or **a lot**
plenty, a great deal, heaps,
loads, many, a large amount,
masses, piles

lovely
a lovely day – pleasant,
glorious, sunny, splendid
a lovely meal – tasty,
scrumptious, delicious
a lovely person – warm, kind,
helpful, friendly
a lovely time – enjoyable,
great, fantastic, wonderful,
fabulous

nasty
a nasty person – unkind,
rude, unpleasant
a nasty taste – horrible, foul,
disgusting, awful

nice
nice food – delicious
a nice person – kind, helpful,
pleasant
a nice view – lovely

Collins Junior Dictionary

Glossary

antennae The feelers on an insect's head.

camouflage How an animal uses its colours to hide.

caterpillar The larva of a butterfly or moth.

cocoon A silk case made by a caterpillar.

insect An animal with six legs and three parts to its body.

metamorphosis When a young insect changes into an adult insect.

nectar Sugary liquid made by flowers.

poisonous Harmful.

pollination When an animal carries pollen from one flower to another. The flower can then make seeds.

proboscis The feeding tube on the head of an insect.

pupa A hard case made from the skin of a larva.

scale A tiny flake on the wing of a butterfly or moth.

shed To get rid of something naturally, such as skin or hair.

shimmer To shine with moving light.

Index

antennae 4, 5, 7, 31

camouflage 26, 27, 31
caterpillars 16–21, 22, 24, 25, 26, 28, 31
cocoon 22, 23, 31
colours 6, 7, 8, 9, 24, 26, 27

eggs 16–17
eye-spots 9, 24

feelers *see* antennae
flowers 12, 14, 15, 22

flying 6, 10–11, 14, 29
food 12–15, 18–19, 28, 29

jaws 16

leaves 16, 17, 18, 19, 26, 29
legs 4, 16

metamorphosis 21, 31

nectar 11, 12, 13, 14, 22, 28, 31

plants 16, 18, 26, 28
poisonous 24, 31
pollen 22
pollination 22, 31
proboscis 12, 13, 14, 31
pupa 20–21, 22, 31

scales 8, 31
shedding 18, 19, 20
silk 22, 23
skin 18, 19, 20

wings 4, 6, 7, 8–9, 10, 14, 20, 21, 23, 26, 27

Butterflies and Moths

Eggs and caterpillars

Butterflies and moths lay their eggs on plants. The eggs hatch into **caterpillars.** A caterpillar looks a bit like a worm. It has three pairs of legs and four pairs of suckers. The legs and suckers help the caterpillar to grip the leaves and stems of plants.

Caterpillar food

Caterpillars start eating as soon as they hatch. They only like certain kinds of leaves. A caterpillar eats all day. It grows so large that its skin gets tight. Then it has to **shed** the old skin and grow a larger one. Sometimes, caterpillars can kill a plant by eating all its leaves.

What is a pupa?

When a caterpillar is fully grown, it stops eating and sheds its skin for the last time. Lying under the old skin is a **pupa.** A pupa is a hard case made from the skin of the caterpillar.

Inside the pupa, the caterpillar slowly changes into an adult butterfly. This is called **metamorphosis.** It means changing shape. Then the pupa splits open and the new adult butterfly comes out.

Sally Morgan

How flowers grow

Most plants grow in the same way. All flowers make seeds from which new plants grow.

Flowers need pollen from other flowers of the same kind before they can make new seeds. Pollen is carried by insects or by the wind.

How seeds are spread

The wind blows some fruits.

Some fruits hook onto animals fur.

Some fruits burst open to throw out seeds.

Birds eat some fruits. Seeds may be passed out in their droppings.

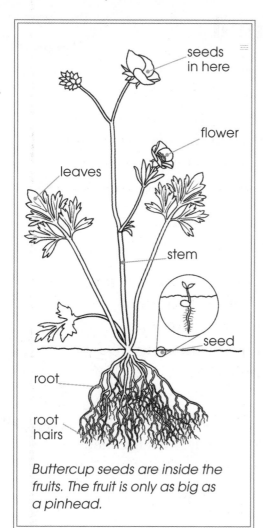

Buttercup seeds are inside the fruits. The fruit is only as big as a pinhead.

- Before it can turn into a new plant, the seed needs water. Rain makes the seed swell. It starts to grow.

- The seed puts out a tiny root with little hairs. The root grows down into the ground.

- The root hairs take in water and minerals from the soil. Soon, a little shoot comes out of the seed.

- The leaves grow. The light helps the plant to make food.

- Later, flowers grow on top of the stalks. They start to make seeds that will grow into other plants.

Book blurbs

Extract 1

This is the story of Max, the hedgehog who becomes a hodgeheg, who becomes a hero!

The hedgehog family of Number 5A are a happy bunch but they dream of reaching the Park. Unfortunately, a very busy road lies between them and their goal and no one has found a way to cross it in safety. No one, that is, until the determined young Max decides to solve the problem once and for all...

A delightfully original animal adventure from a master storyteller.

Dick King-Smith was born near Bristol. After serving in the Grenadier Guards during the Second World War, he spent twenty years as a farmer in Gloucestershire, an experience which inspired many of his stories. He went on to teach at a village primary school. His first book, *The Fox Busters,* was published in 1978. Since then he has written a great number of children's books, including *The Sheep-Pig* (winner of the *Guardian* Award), *Harry's Mad, Noah's Brother, The Hodgeheg, Martin's Mice, Ace, The Cuckoo Child* and many others. He is married with three children and ten grandchildren, and lives in Avon.

Extract 2

Pat is a young sea otter who never stops asking questions – although she doesn't always listen to the answers! Life can be dangerous for a young otter, though, and Pat quickly learns how to deal with hungry sharks and sudden storms. Then, one day, Pat has a Great Adventure – and it is so exciting that she almost forgets to ask any questions!

Another wonderful character from the author of the very popular *The Owl Who Was Afraid of the Dark.*
There are lots more animals to meet in this delightful series by Jill Tomlinson:
The Aardvark Who Wasn't Sure
The Cat Who Wanted to Go Home
The Gorilla Who Wanted to Grow Up

Story openings

Extract 1

The Hodgeheg

"YOUR AUNTIE BETTY has copped it," said Pa Hedgehog to Ma.

"Oh, no!" cried Ma. "Where?"

"Just down the road. Opposite the newsagent's. Bad place to cross, that."

"Everywhere's a bad place to cross nowadays," said Ma. "The traffic's dreadful. Do you realise, Pa, that's the third this year, and all on my side of the family too. First there was Grandfather, then my second cousin once removed, and now poor old Auntie Betty…"

Extract 2

The Otter Who Wanted to Know

Pat was a young sea otter. She was rolling over and over in the sea, washing her fur. She gave it a final wash. Then she lay on her back, turned up her toes and the tip of her broad tail, and floated on the sea for a rest.

Bobby was a sea otter too. He had just noticed Pat for the first time. Although she was small she seemed to know how to look after herself. He went over to her.

"Hello," he said. "What are you doing?"

Pat kept her eyes shut. "Nothing," she said. She knew better than to talk to strange otters.

Bobby paddled round beside her, and lay on the water too.

"Good," he said, "I've got nothing to do either, so I'll do it with you."

"The sea's quite big," said Pat. "There's plenty of room for both of us."

"Yes, it is big," Bobby said. But he wasn't going to be put off as easily as that. "It's called the Pacific, you know."

"I didn't know that," Pat said, interested at once. "Why?"

❶ Dick King-Smith ❷ Jill Tomlinson

Scene setting

Extract 1

The Hodgeheg

They were sitting in a flower-bed at their home, the garden of Number 5A of a row of semi-detached houses in a suburban street. On the other side of the road was a Park, very popular with local hedgehogs on account of the good hunting it offered. As well as worms and slugs and snails, which they could find in their own gardens, there were special attractions in the Park. Mice lived under the Bandstand, feasting on the crumbs dropped from listeners' sandwiches; frogs dwelt in the Lily-Pond, and in the Ornamental Gardens grass-snakes slithered through the shrubbery. All these creatures were regarded as great delicacies by the hedgehogs, and they could never resist the occasional night's sport in the Park. But to reach it, they had to cross the busy road.

Extract 2

The Otter Who Wanted to Know

"I can manage mussels," Pat said, "but I don't think I could open one of those oysters."

"There may not be any oysters left to open soon," said Bobby.

"Why shouldn't there be any left?" asked Pat.

"Because there are so many of us," said Bobby, "that it's getting harder and harder to find food."

"No one else seems to have found this place," Pat said. "Let's go and hunt for some more, and this time I'll see if I can break one myself."

They dived among the rocks. They looked and looked, and felt with their paws. Finally they each found one rock oyster. They had to come up to the surface of the water to breathe again.

Characterisation

Extract 1

The Hodgeheg

Almost from the moment his eyes had opened, while his prickles were still soft and rubbery, Max had shown promise of being a bright boy; and by now his eyes, his ears, and his wits were all as sharp as his spines.

"What are you talking about, Ma?" he said.

"Nothing," said Ma hastily.

"You wouldn't be talking about nothing," said Max, "or there wouldn't be any point in talking."

Max listened carefully. Then he said, "Do humans cross the road?"

"I suppose so," said Pa.

"But don't they get killed?"

"Don't think so," said Pa. "Never seen one lying in the road. Which I would have if they did."

"Well then," said Max, "how do they get across safely?"

"You tell me, son. You tell me," said Pa.

" I will," said Max. "I will."

Extract 2

The Otter Who Wanted to Know

Bobby didn't reply. He was looking at the sky.

"I don't like the look of that," he said. "Those are storm clouds and the sea is getting choppy. We must get farther out to sea."

"Why?" asked Pat.

"Because the waves will smash us against the rocks!"

"I can't see any waves," said Pat. "I'm going back to that place we found yesterday. I fancy another rock oyster."

"No, you mustn't," said Bobby. "That's just where the waves will begin!"

But he was too late. Pat wasn't listening. She had gone round to the inlet and was under the water hunting for oysters. She found one. But when she came up with it she couldn't lie still to smash it, because the waves were breaking over the rocks. They nearly threw her onto a sharp edge.

① Dick King-Smith ② Jill Tomlinson

Little Red Riding Pig

Cycling through a forest glade, she met a wolf.

"Hold it right there, baby," said the wolf.

Little Red Riding Pig held it.

"Where you headin'?" said the wolf.

"To visit my grandmother," replied Little Red Riding Pig.

The wolf thought quickly. Not a lot of meat on this piglet, he said to himself, but the granny – now she might make a square meal.

"Your granny kinda fat?" he asked in a casual way.

"Oh yes!" said Little Red Riding Pig. "She's very fat."

"Sure like to meet her," said the wolf. "She live around here some place?"

"Oh yes!" said Little Red Riding Pig, and she told the wolf how to get to her grandmother's house, and away he went.

When he arrived, he knocked on the door and a voice called, "Come in, my dear," so he did.

There, lying in bed, was the fattest pig the wolf had ever seen.

"Goodness me!" said the pig. "I thought you were my little granddaughter."

"'Fraid not ma'am," said the wolf.

"But I see now," said Little Red Riding Pig's grandmother, "that you are in fact a handsome stranger. What big ears you have!"

All the better to hear you with, thought the wolf, but he kept his mouth shut.

"And what big eyes you have!"

All the better to see you with, thought the wolf, but he said nothing, merely opening his jaws in a kind of silent laugh.

"And what big teeth you have!" said the fat pig, and before the wolf could think about that, she went on, "Which reminds me, I have the toothache. I should be so grateful if you could look and see which tooth is causing the trouble."

Dick King-Smith

The Really Ugly Duckling

Once upon a time there was a mother duck and a father duck
who had seven baby ducklings. Six of them were regular-looking
ducklings. The seventh was a really ugly duckling.
Everyone used to say, "What a nice-looking bunch of
ducklings—all except that one. Boy, he's really ugly." The really
ugly duckling heard these people, but he didn't care. He knew
that one day he would probably grow up to be a swan and be
bigger and look better than anything in the pond.

Well, as it turned out, he was just a really ugly duckling. And he grew up to be just a really ugly duck. The End.

Jon Scieszka

A Big Bare Bear

A big bare bear
>bought a bear balloon,

For a big bear trip
>to the bare, bare moon.

A hairy bear
>saw the bare bear fly

On the big bear trip
>in the bare, bare sky.

The hairy bear
>took a jet up high

To catch the bear
>in the big bare sky.

The hairy bear
>flew his jet right by

The bear balloon
>in the big bare sky.

He popped the balloon
>with his hairy thumb,

And the bare bear fell
>on his big bum bum.

Robert Heidbreder

On the Ning Nang Nong

On the Ning Nang Nong
Where the Cows go Bong!
And the Monkeys all say Boo!
There's a Nong Nang Ning
Where the trees go Ping!
And the teapots Jibber Jabber Joo.
On the Nong Ning Nang
All the mice go Clang!
And you just can't catch 'em when they do!
So it's Ning Nang Nong!
Cows go Bong!
Nong Nang Ning!
Trees go Ping!
Nong Ning Nang!
The mice go Clang!
What a noisy place to belong,
Is the Ning Nang Ning Nang Nong!!

Spike Milligan

Sneezles

Christopher Robin
Had wheezles
And sneezles,
They bundled him
Into
His bed.
They gave him what goes
With a cold in the nose,
And some more for a cold
In the head.
They wondered
If wheezles
Could turn
Into measles,
If sneezles
Would turn
Into mumps;
They examined his chest
For a rash,
And the rest
Of his body for swellings and lumps.
They sent for some doctors
In sneezles
And wheezles
To tell them what ought
To be done.
All sorts and conditions
Of famous physicians
Came hurrying round
At a run.
They all made a note

Of the state of his throat,
They asked if he suffered from thirst;
They asked if the sneezles
Came *after* the wheezles,
Or if the first sneezle
Came first.
They said, "If you teazle
A sneezle
Or wheezle,
A measle
May easily grow.
But humour or pleazle
The wheezle
Or sneezle,
The measle will certainly go."
They expounded the reazles
For sneezles
And wheezles,
The manner of measles
When new.
They said "If he freezles
In draughts and in breezles,
Then PHTHEEZLES
May even ensue."

Christopher Robin
Got up in the morning,
The sneezles had vanished away.
And the look in his eye
Seemed to say to the sky,
"Now, how to amuse them to-day?"

AA Milne

Busy Day

Pop in
pop out
pop over the road
pop out for a walk
pop in for a talk
pop down to the shop
can't stop
got to pop

got to pop?

pop where?
pop what?

well
I've got to
pop round
pop up
pop in to town
pop out and see
pop in for tea
pop down to the shop
can't stop
got to pop

got to pop?

pop where?
pop what?

well
I've got to
pop in
pop out
pop over the road
pop out for a walk
pop in for a talk…

Michael Rosen

Limericks

❶

There was an Old Man with a beard,
Who said, "It is just as I feared! –
    Two Owls and a Hen,
    four Larks and a Wren,
Have all built their nests in my beard!"

Edward Lear

❷

I have a strange Auntie called Jean.
She's quite tall and thin as a bean.
On bright sunny days,
When she's standing sideways,
Aunt Jean cannot even be seen.

John Kitching

❸

A bald-headed man from Dundee
Lost his wig, in a wind, in a tree;
When he looked up and spied it,
A hen was inside it,
And it laid him an egg for his tea.

Jack Ousbey

❹

There was a small maiden named Maggie,
Whose dog was enormous and shaggy;
The front end of him
Looked vicious and grim –
But the tail end was friendly and waggy.

Anon

❺

There was an old man of Peru,
Who dreamt he was eating his shoe.
    He woke in the night
    In a terrible fright,
And found it was perfectly true.

Anon

Teaser

What kind of ants
tear down trees?
What kind of ants
roll in mud
to take their ease?
What kind of ants
have four knees?
What kind of ants
flap their ears
in the breeze?
What kind of ants
spell their name
with two 'e's?
Sh! Don't tell.
It's a tease.

Tony Mitton

Answer: Elephants

Barry and Beryl the Bubble Gum Blowers

Barry and Beryl the bubble gum blowers
blew bubble gum bubbles as big as balloons.
All shapes and sizes, zebras and zeppelins,
swordfish and sealions, sharks and baboons,
babies and buckets, bottles and biplanes,
buffaloes, bees, trombones and bassoons
Barry and Beryl the bubble gum blowers
blew bubble gum bubbles as big as balloons.

Barry and Beryl the bubble gum blowers
blew bubble gum bubbles all over the place.
Big ones in bed, on backseats of buses,
blowing their bubbles in baths with bad taste,
they blew and they bubbled from breakfast till bedtime
the biggest gum bubble that history traced.
One last big breath… and the bubble exploded
bursting and blasting their heads into space.
Yes, Barry and Beryl the bubble gum blowers
blew bubbles that blasted their heads into space.

Paul Cookson

Fact or Fiction?

❶

CONTENTS

1 Questions, questions,
   questions   *Page* 9

2 Playing 'dead'   18

3 Sharks!   27

4 Pat meets the Gaffer   36

5 Rescue by Man   46

6 In the swim   54

7 Together again   63

8 Journey by air   68

9 Return to the sea   75

❷

CONTENTS

Toothed whales 5

Beluga 6

Narwhal 8

Sperm whale 10

Dolphins and porpoises...... 12

River dolphins....................... 14

Porpoises 16

Beaked whales 18

Bottlenose whales 20

❸

INDEX

Amazon river dolphin
    14, 15

baleen whales 5,
    22–23
beaked whales 18–19
beluga 6–7
black right whale 23,
    34, 35, 36
blow hole 10
blubber 36
blue whales 5, 26–27,
    36
bottlenose or barrel-
    headed whales 20–21

Bryde's whale 32

communication 6

dolphins 5, 12–13, 14–15

echolocation 7, 14
endangered whales 6,
    8, 12, 21, 36, 37

feeding 6, 8, 10, 11, 12,
    13, 14, 15, 18, 20, 22,
    24, 26, 28, 30, 31
feeding young 5, 6
finless porpoise 16

Dolphins and Porpoises

Dolphins are toothed whales with beak-like jaws, a pair of large V-shaped flippers and usually a well-developed curved fin on the back. They feed mainly on fish, squid and octopuses. There are 31 species of dolphin.

Porpoises are the smallest of the toothed whales, growing to about 1.5 metres (5 feet) in length. They have a rounded, beakless face with jaws armed with stubby or spade-like teeth. The fin on the back, if they have one, is small and triangular in shape. Porpoises feed primarily on fish. There are only six species.

Both dolphins and porpoises live close to land and this brings them in contact with people. Unfortunately, this results in many of them being killed for food, trapped in fishing nets, or poisoned by sea pollution. They are friendly animals, playing with swimmers and divers in shallow water and swimming alongside boats. They are also intelligent, having a language of whistles, chirps, clicks and moans which they use to 'talk' to one another and communicate with people.

A distinctive shape
It is easy to tell dolphins and porpoises apart as they have very different body shapes or outlines.

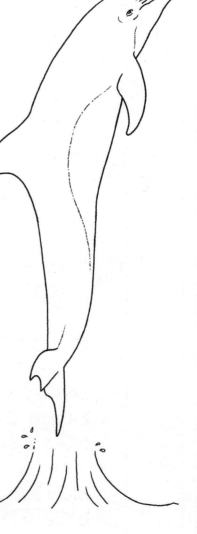

Lionel Bender

OUR SOLAR SYSTEM

The Solar System is made up of the Sun and all the objects that spin around it.

The Sun
The Sun is a star – that is, a massive ball of exploding gases. It applies a pulling force, called gravity, to everything nearby. This keeps objects in their places, going around and around the Sun.

The planets
The largest things that spin around the Sun are the planets. The Earth is one of the planets. Scientists have discovered nine planets so far.

Great and small
The biggest planet is called Jupiter, followed by Saturn. The smallest planet is Pluto.

Asteroids
Asteroids are large chunks of rock, or rock and metal. They are dotted all over the Solar System. However, most of them lie between Jupiter and Mars in a band called the Asteroid Belt.

Moons
Many planets have moons going around them. The Earth has only one moon, but some planets have more. For example, Saturn has at least 18 moons.

Most moons are balls of rock and ice. Many have craters, mountains and valleys. One of Jupiter's moons may even have an ocean.

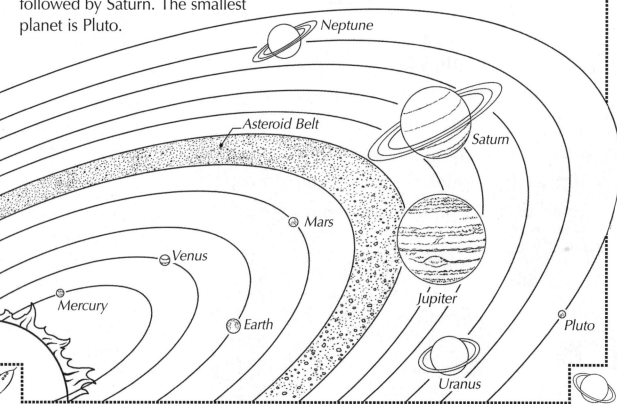

Neptune

Asteroid Belt

Saturn

Mars

Venus

Jupiter

Mercury

Earth

Pluto

Uranus

PUSHING AND PULLING

A force is a push or a pull. You cannot see a force, but you can see and feel its effects. You see the effect of the wind's force as leaves move on a tree, or feel its effect as the air pushes against your skin.

The force of the wind is making these trees bend.

EXERTING FORCES

The word *exerted* is used to describe how a force is made. We say that the wind exerts a force when it blows the leaves. You exert a force on this page when you hold it.

Pushes and pulls move things. Once something is moving, a pull or a push may be exerted to change its direction and speed – or to stop it altogether. For example, you may use a bat to change the direction of a ball that is thrown to you.

These children are using their muscles, exerting a force to pick up these containers.

MOVEMENT

Without forces there would be no movement. When muscles work, they exert forces that pull on your bones and move your limbs, letting you run, walk and swim. Engines exert forces to move cars, trucks, ships, submarines and spacecraft.

Text: Peter D Riley; Images © Ken Kaup/SODA and © Corbis/Digital Stock

Acknowledgements

The publishers gratefully acknowledge permission to reproduce the following copyright material:

Bloomsbury Publishing for 'Word of a Lie' from *The Frog Who Dreamed She Was an Opera Singer* by Jackie Kay © 1998, Jackie Kay (1998, Bloomsbury Publishing). **Chrysalis Books** for extracts from *Butterflies and Moths* by Sally Morgan © 2000, Sally Morgan (2000, Chrysalis Children's Books). **Paul Cookson** for 'Barry and Beryl the Bubblegum Blowers' by Paul Cookson from *Tongue Twisters and Tonsil Twizzlers* © 1997, Paul Cookson (1997, Macmillan). **June Crebbin** for 'Dinner-time Rhyme' from *Jungle Sale* by June Crebbin © 1988, June Crebbin (1988, Viking Kestrel). **Curtis Brown Group Ltd** for 'Morning' from *Give Yourself a Hug* by Grace Nichols © 1994, Grace Nichols (1994, A&C Black). **Egmont Books** for extracts from *The Helen Oxenbury Nursery Story Book* retold by Helen Oxenbury © 1985, Helen Oxenbury (1985, William Heinemann Limited); for 'Happiness' by AA Milne from *When We Were Very Young* by AA Milne © 1924, AA Milne (1924, Methuen); for an extract from *But you promised!* by Bel Mooney © 1990, Bel Mooney (1990, Egmont Books); for 'The End' and 'Sneezles' by AA Milne from *Now We Are Six* by AA Milne © 1927, AA Milne (1927, Methuen); for extracts from *The Otter Who Wanted to Know* by Jill Tomlinson © 1979, Jill Tomlinson (1979, Methuen); for an extract from *Frog and Toad Together* by Arnold Lobel © 1973, Arnold Lobel (1973, World's Work). **Era Publications** for 'Felt finger puppets' from *Making Puppets* by Josie McKinnon © 1993, Josie McKinnon (1993, Era Publications, Australia). **Fitzhenry and Whiteside Publishers** for 'A Big Bare Bear' from *Don't Eat Spiders* by Robert Heidbreder © 1985, Robert Heidbreder (1985, OUP Canada). **John Foster** for 'I'm not scared of the monster' from *Bare Bear and other rhymes* compiled by John Foster © 1999, John Foster (1999, Oxford University Press). **HarperCollins Publishers Limited** for extracts from *Collins Junior Dictionary* © 2000, HarperCollins (2000, HarperCollins). **David Higham Associates** for 'Dad' by Berlie Doherty from *Walking on Air* by Berlie Doherty © 1993, Berlie Doherty (1993, HarperCollins); for an extract from *The Magic Finger* by Roald Dahl © 1968, Roald Dahl (1968, Allen & Unwin). **Houghton Mifflin Company** for 'The Little Red Hen and the Grain of Wheat' from *Stories to Tell Children* retold by Sara Cone Bryant © Sara Cone Bryant (Houghton Mifflin Company). **Kingfisher** for 'The Rare Spotted Birthday Party' by Margaret Mahy © 1989, Margaret Mahy (© 1989, Kingfisher). **John Kitching** for 'Family Problems' from *The Works* chosen by Paul Cookson © 2000, John Kitching (2000, Macmillan); for 'Don't' from *Twinkle Twinkle Chocolate Bar* compiled by John Foster © 1991, John Kitching (1991, Oxford University Press). **Wes Magee** for 'What is the sun?' from *Read a poem, write a poem* by Wes Magee © 1989, Wes Magee (1989, Basil Blackwell). **Marilyn Malin** for 'Rabbit and Tiger' from *Cric Crac* by Grace Hallworth © 1990, Grace Hallworth (1990, Methuen). **Spike Milligan Productions Limited** for 'On the Ning Nang Nong' from *Silly Verses for Kids* by Spike Milligan © 1968, Spike Milligan (1968, Penguin). **Tony Mitton** for 'Teaser' from *The Works* chosen by Paul Cookson © 2000, Tony Mitton (2000, Macmillan). **Pamela Mordecai** for 'Caribbean Counting Rhyme' by Pamela Mordecai from *Sunjet* published by Air Jamaica. **Orion Publishing Group Limited** for an extract from 'Little Red Riding Pig' from *Dick King-Smith's Triffic Pig Book* © 1991, Dick King-Smith (© 1991, Victor Gollancz Limited). **Jack Ousbey** for 'A bald-headed man from Dundee' from *The Works* chosen by Paul Cookson © 2000, Jack Ousbey (2000, Macmillan). **Penguin Group UK** for an extract from *The Werepuppy on Holiday* by Jacqueline Wilson © 1994, Jacqueline Wilson (1994, Blackie); for 'The Really Ugly Duckling' from *The Stinky Cheese Man and Other Fairly Stupid Tales* by Jon Scieszka and Lane Smith © 1992, Jon Scieszka (1992, Viking). **The Peters Fraser and Dunlop Group** for 'Busy Day' by Michael Rosen from *You Tell Me* by Michael Rosen © 1979, Michael Rosen (1979, Kestrel). **Random House Group** for extracts from 'Brer Rabbit and the Tar Baby' from *The Tales of Uncle Remus* retold by Julius Lester © 1987, Julius Lester (1987, Bodley Head). **Reading and Language Information Centre** for an extract from *Children making books* by Paul Johnson © 1995, Paul Johnson (1995, Reading and Language Information Centre). **Scholastic Children's Books Limited** for extracts from *The Book of Whales, Dolphins and Porpoises* by Lionel Bender © 1992, Lionel Bender (© 1992, Scholastic Children's Books Limited); for 'Conversation' from *Wouldn't You Like to Know* by Michael Rosen © 1977, Michael Rosen (© 1977, André Deutsche). **Usborne Publishing** for an extract from *Finding Out About Everyday Things* by Eliot Humberstone © 1981, Eliot Humberstone (1981, Usborne Publishing); for an extract from *Our Solar System* by Alistair Smith © 1998, Alistair Smith (1998, Usborne). **Barrie Wade** for 'Come-day Go-day' from *Twinkle Twinkle Chocolate Bar* compiled by John Foster © 1991, Barrie Wade (1991, Oxford University Press). **AP Watt Ltd** for extracts from *The Hodgeheg* by Dick King-Smith © 1987, Dick King-Smith (1987, Hamish Hamilton). **The Watts Publishing Group** for an extract from *Straightforward Science: Forces and Movement* by Peter Riley © 1998, Peter Riley (1998, Franklin Watts). **Bernard Young** for 'Best Friends' from *Poems about you and me* compiled by Brian Moses © 1998, Bernard Young (1998, Wayland).

Every effort has been made to trace copyright holders for the works reproduced in this book, and the publishers apologise for any inadvertent omissions.